Viva HA

Covers models from 1963 to 1966

Owners Handbook/Maintenance Manual

by D H Stead

HAYNES

1862/059

Acknowledgements

Thanks are due to many people for their
help and enthusiasm in the prduction of
this handbook.

Further thanks are extended to the manufacturer of the Viva for the use of certain
illustrations and to Castrol Limited.

A handbook in the Haynes Owners Handbook
and Maintenance Manual Series.

Edited by Tim Parker and Stanley Randolph

Published by J H Haynes and Company Limited,
Sparkford, Yeovil, Somerset.

Set in 10 point IBM Univers Medium

Printed in England

SBN no 90055 059 7

Contents

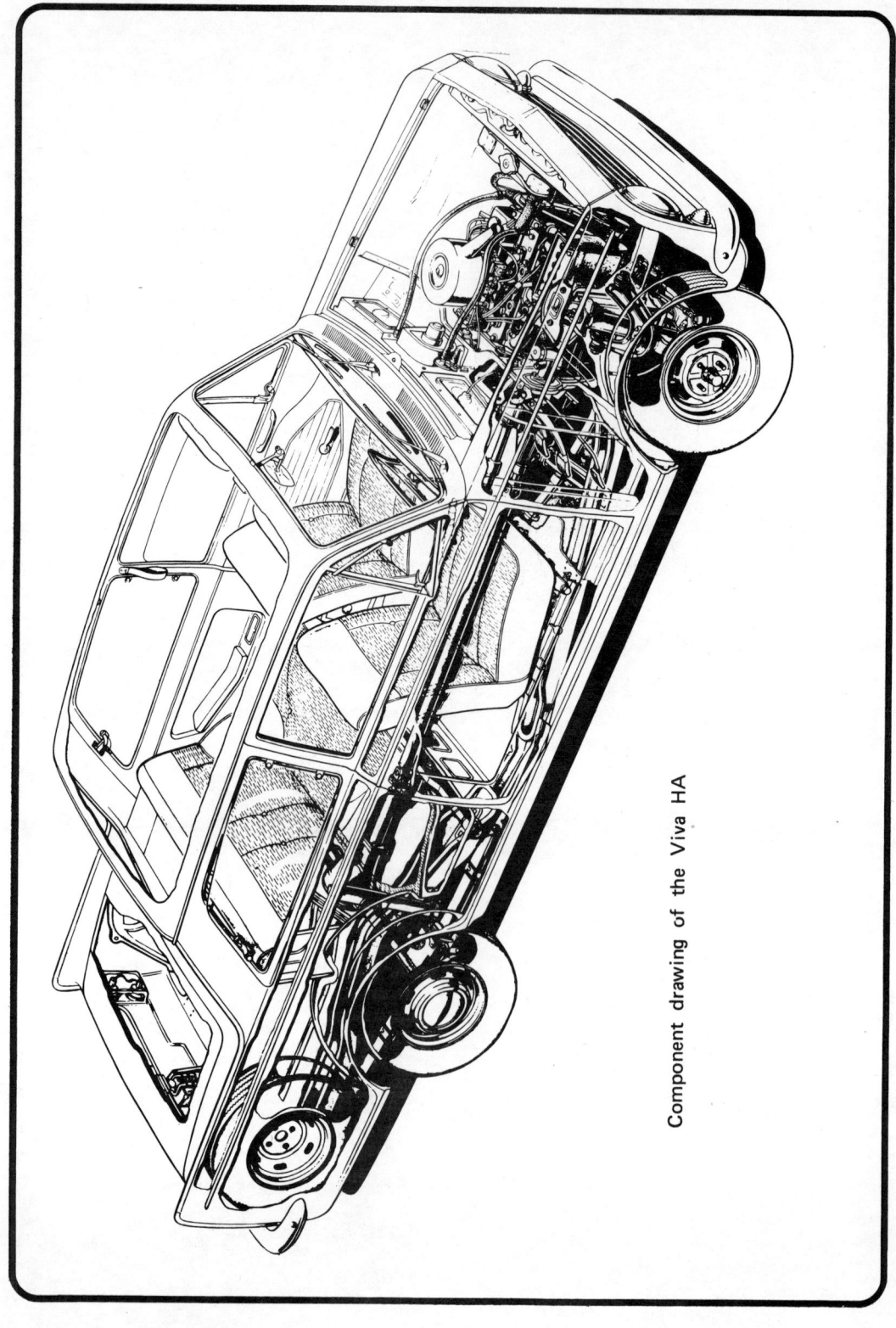

Component drawing of the Viva HA

Introduction

This handbook has a specific purpose. To tell you enough about your Viva so that you know what it can do in terms of economy and performance; you know what you must do in order to keep that economy and performance; and know what to do to get the car going again if it should fail when you could be a long way from home.

You will also be shown how to examine your Viva to check that all is well. Examination is the larger part of maintenance on the modern car, so many parts are 'sealed - no lubrication necessary' that people tend to forget that these parts still wear out.

The car examination will deal with all items that the MOT examiner will also look at.

It will also provide a good guide to condition if you are contemplating buying a secondhand Viva.

If you know but little of cars and anyway have little time to spend worrying about them, this handbook should enable you to get some idea of what goes on and to understand your garage bills. For the more knowledgeable it will provide the particular information necessary for the correct servicing, repair, fault finding and rectification applicable specifically to the Vauxhall Viva.

As with all cars, there is one simple unalterable fact which many people either do not know, do not **want** to know, or ignore. If you want safety, reliability and economy, time **must** be set aside for regular and proper maintenance and attention.

A number of people worry, understandably, about the state of their car. Particularly when it has cost hundreds of pounds. We hope this handbook will help to alleviate most of this worry by giving you an idea of the condition of the car you may just be about to buy and what is needed to keep it from causing worry during your ownership. It has been compiled by a Viva owner for the benefit of other Viva owners.

After successfully using this handbook, should you wish to tackle the more complicated type of repair a most useful Owner's Workshop Manual is available on the Viva HA direct from the publishers or through all good accessory shops and booksellers.

Viva SL

Model identification

The Viva HA and its versions was manufactured from September 1963 to September 1966. (The van only is still in production). The total range was superseded by the 'coke bottle' Viva HB in September 1966.

The first of the Vivas was Vauxhall's move into the small car market where they had never really been before, except for the old 'Ten' which disappeared in 1947. The car was designed to provide cheap and economical transport. The bodyshell is boxy and functional and all models in the range were two door. The body was suspended on a transverse leaf spring at the front and semi-elliptic leaf springs at the rear.

A new four cylinder ohv engine of 1057 cc capacity was designed for the car. A gearbox with four forward speeds all fitted with synchromesh was used and the bodywork was painted in an acrylic lacquer which needed no polishing (in theory).

The initial models were the Standard and De Luxe. The latter was fitted with a heater and screen washer as standard, being optional extras otherwise. The De Luxe version had carpets and other interior and exterior trim refinements.

In June 1965 an SL version (Super Luxury) was introduced. This had aluminium grilles and more exterior trim and the seats were more luxurious. The facia panel was also altered. In July 1965 the Standard and De Luxe models were fitted with amber flashers and the sidelamps were incorporated in the headlamps. In October 1965 the De Luxe 90 and SL 90 versions were introduced. These were fitted with uprated engines with a higher compression ratio and a Stromberg 150 CD carburettor. Servo assisted disc brakes on the front wheels were also fitted as standard.

A Bedford van version of the car was also produced (and still is, with the later engines fitted to the original body design) in 1964. This comes in 6 cwt or 8 cwt load capacities, the heavier load version having uprated rear springs. An estate version of the HAV Van is called the 'Bedford Beagle'. These vans and estate vehicles are marketed under the Bedford name but are of the same family as the Viva HA whose identification letters they take. Servicing procedures are the same.

Models

HAS	2 door Standard Saloon
HAD	2 door De Luxe Saloon
HAD21	2 door De Luxe 90 Saloon
HAH	2 door SL Saloon
HAA21	2 door SL90 Saloon
HAE	6 cwt Van
HAV	8 cwt Van and Beagle

The model and chassis numbers on all models are to be found on a plate fitted to the left side of the dash panel under the bonnet. The engine number is stamped on the side of the cylinder block just underneath the front spark plug.

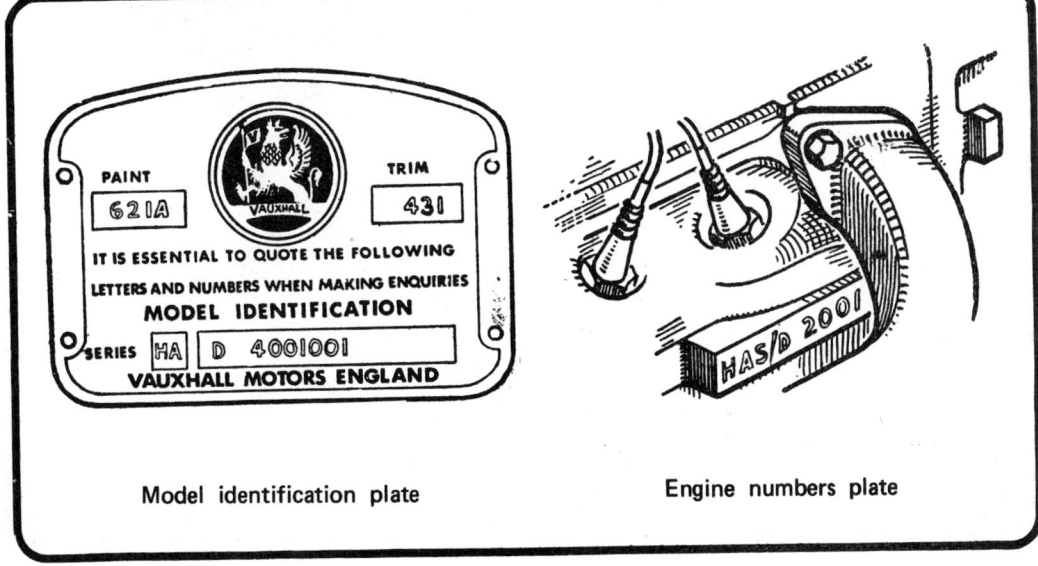

Model identification plate   Engine numbers plate

Viva HA

Bedford 6 cwt Van

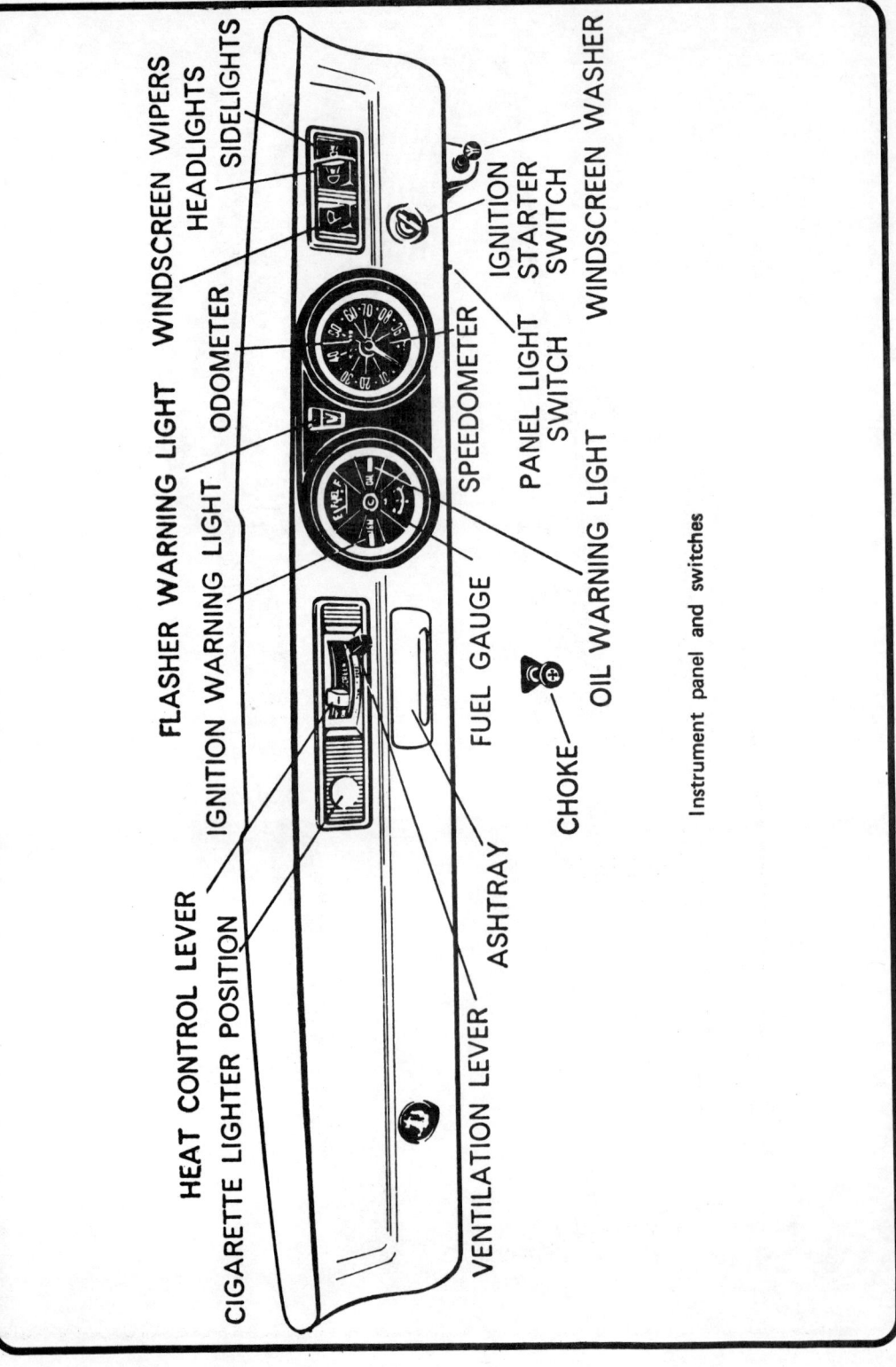

WINDSCREEN WASHER

IGNITION STARTER SWITCH

WINDSCREEN WIPERS

HEADLIGHTS

SIDELIGHTS

FLASHER WARNING LIGHT

IGNITION WARNING LIGHT

ODOMETER

SPEEDOMETER

PANEL LIGHT SWITCH

OIL WARNING LIGHT

FUEL GAUGE

CHOKE

HEAT CONTROL LEVER

CIGARETTE LIGHTER POSITION

VENTILATION LEVER

ASHTRAY

Instrument panel and switches

Specifications, dimensions, weights and capacities

Engine   4 cylinder in line ohv, pushrod operated

Piston displacement   1057 cc (64.5 cu in)
  Bore   74.3 mm (2.925 in)
  Stroke   60.96 mm (2.40 in)

Firing order   1 3 4 2
Gross bhp
   Standard engine 7.3:1 compression ratio 47.8 at 5,200 rpm
   Standard engine 8.5:1 compression ratio 50.1 at 5,200 rpm
   90 engine 9.0:1 compression ratio   60.1 at 5,400 rpm

Torque figures   8.5:1 CR   7.3:1 CR
  net   59.1 lb ft at 2800 rpm   55.0 lb ft at 2600 rpm

Cooling system
  Type   Thermosyphon assisted by impeller pump driven by the fan belt
  Capacity   10¼ pints — with heater 11¼ pints
  Blow off pressure (radiator filler cap) 6¼ - 7¾ lb/sq in
  Fan   Metal - four bladed
  Fan belt tension   Depression of ½ inch under 9 lbs pressure midway between fan and generator pulleys

Fuel System
Fuel is drawn from the 7 gallon under boot floor storage tank by an AC mechanical pump driven by an eccentric in the camshaft. The pump delivers it to a fixed choke downdraught carburettor (or variable choke side draught carburettor) on 90 high performance engines

  Fuel pump pressure   1½ - 2½ lb/sq in
  Fuel octane requirement   97 (8.5:1 CR)
                                                    90 (7.3:1 CR)
  Carburettor make (fixed choke)   Solex B30 PSEI
          (variable choke) Stromberg 150 CD

Ignition System
12 v coil and distributor with automatic centrifugal and vacuum advance controls

Distributor type   Delco-Remy D202

Contact points gap   .020 in (.51 mm)
  Ignition timing (static)   9° BTDC
  Timing marks   On crankshaft pulley and timing gear cover

Spark plugs
  Type   AC42XLS
  Gap   .030 in (.76 mm)

Clutch
  Make   Borg and Beck
  Type   Single plate diaphragm spring. Clutch release controlled by cable
  Cable adjustment   ¼ inch free play between cable end and operating lever
  Diameter   6¼ inch

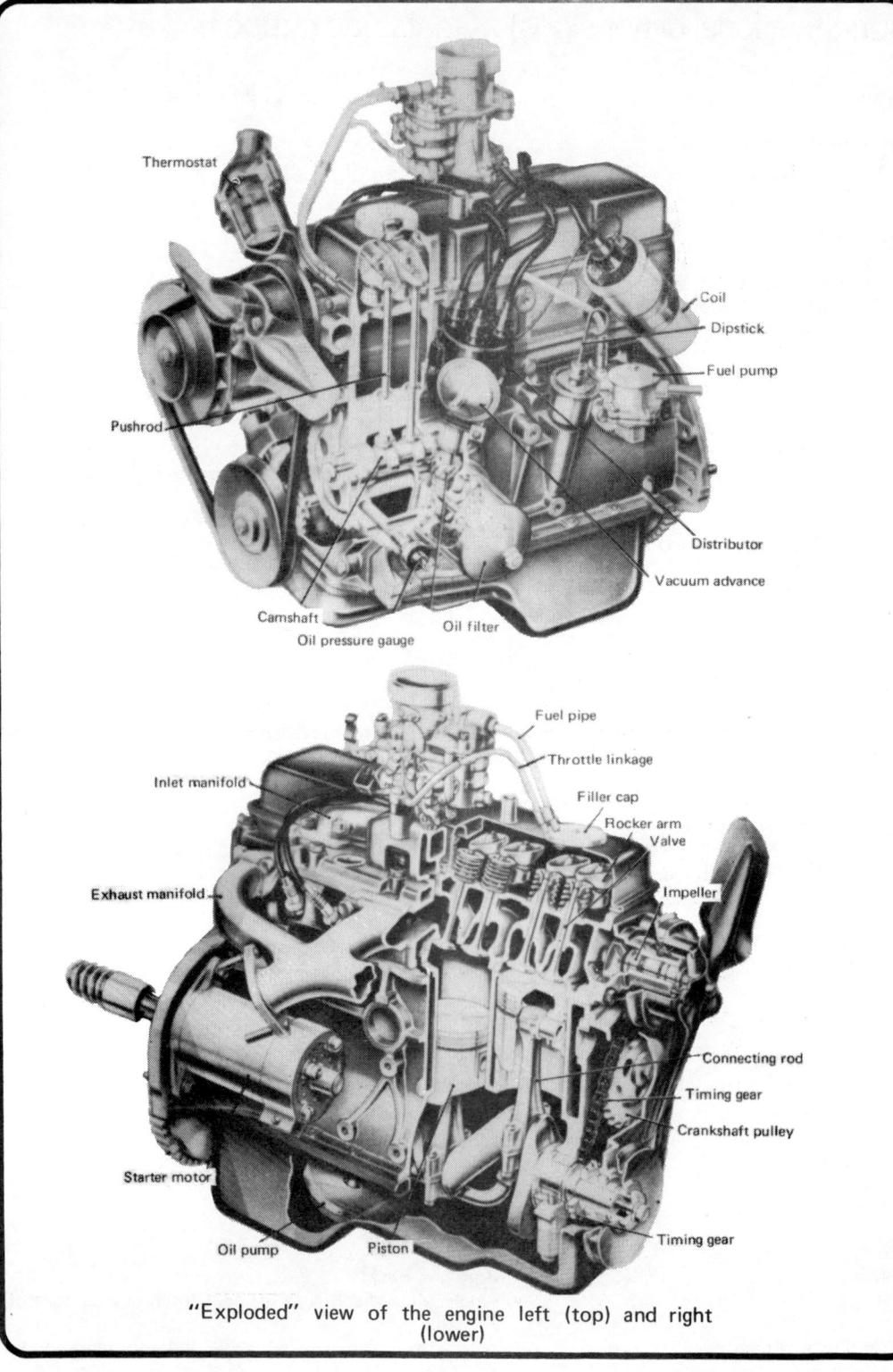

Thermostat

Coil

Dipstick

Fuel pump

Pushrod

Distributor

Vacuum advance

Camshaft

Oil pressure gauge

Oil filter

Fuel pipe

Throttle linkage

Inlet manifold

Filler cap

Rocker arm

Valve

Exhaust manifold

Impeller

Connecting rod

Timing gear

Crankshaft pulley

Starter motor

Oil pump

Piston

Timing gear

"Exploded" view of the engine left (top) and right (lower)

Gearbox

Four forward speeds with synchromesh on all forward gears. One reverse.

Ratios
1st	3.765:1
2nd	2.213:1
3rd	1.404:1
4th	1.000:1
Reverse	3.707:1

Rear Axle

Semi-floating, live with hypoid bevel pinion drive

Ratios	4.125:1
	3.89:1 (optional)

Overall Gear Ratios

Overall gear ratios may be calculated by the use of the following equation:

Gear ratio x rear axle ratio = overall gear ratio

Steering

Type	Rack and pinion
Ratio	to September 1964 18:1 September 1964 on 16:1
Steering wheel turns (lock to lock)	3.79 (up to 1964) 3.14 (September 1964 on)
Turning circle	29 ft

Steering geometry

Front wheel alignment	.08 - .14 in to in
Camber angle	$\frac{1}{4}^{\circ}$ to 1°
King pin (steering pivot) inclination	7° to 8°
Castor angle	$\frac{1}{4}^{\circ}$ to 3°

Front suspension

Independent, double wishbone with transverse leaf spring and telescopic hydraulic dampers mounted vertically through the upper wishbone.

Rear suspension

Semi-elliptic leaf springs mounted on bodyframe side rails on rubber bushed pins and shackles. Special spring to axle mountings with an additional crossmember to support the downward stresses on the pinion extension. Two telescopic hydraulic dampers are mounted at an angle from the spring seats to brackets on the underframe.

Tyres and pressures

Standard tyres fitted (saloons)	5.50 x 12 (4 ply)
(vans)	5.50 x 12 (6 ply)
Wheels	Pressed steel disc wheels 4 stud fixing 4J x 12

Pressures

	Front	Rear
Saloons - normal conditions	18 lb/sq in	22 lb/sq in
Saloons - prolonged speed or max loads	22 lb/sq in	26 lb/sq in
Van HAE - normal	20 lb/sq in	36 lb/sq in
HAE - prolonged speed or max loads	20 lb/sq in	40 lb/sq in
Van HAV - normal	20 lb/sq in	40 lb/sq in
HAV - prolonged speed or max load	20 lb/sq in	45 lb/sq in

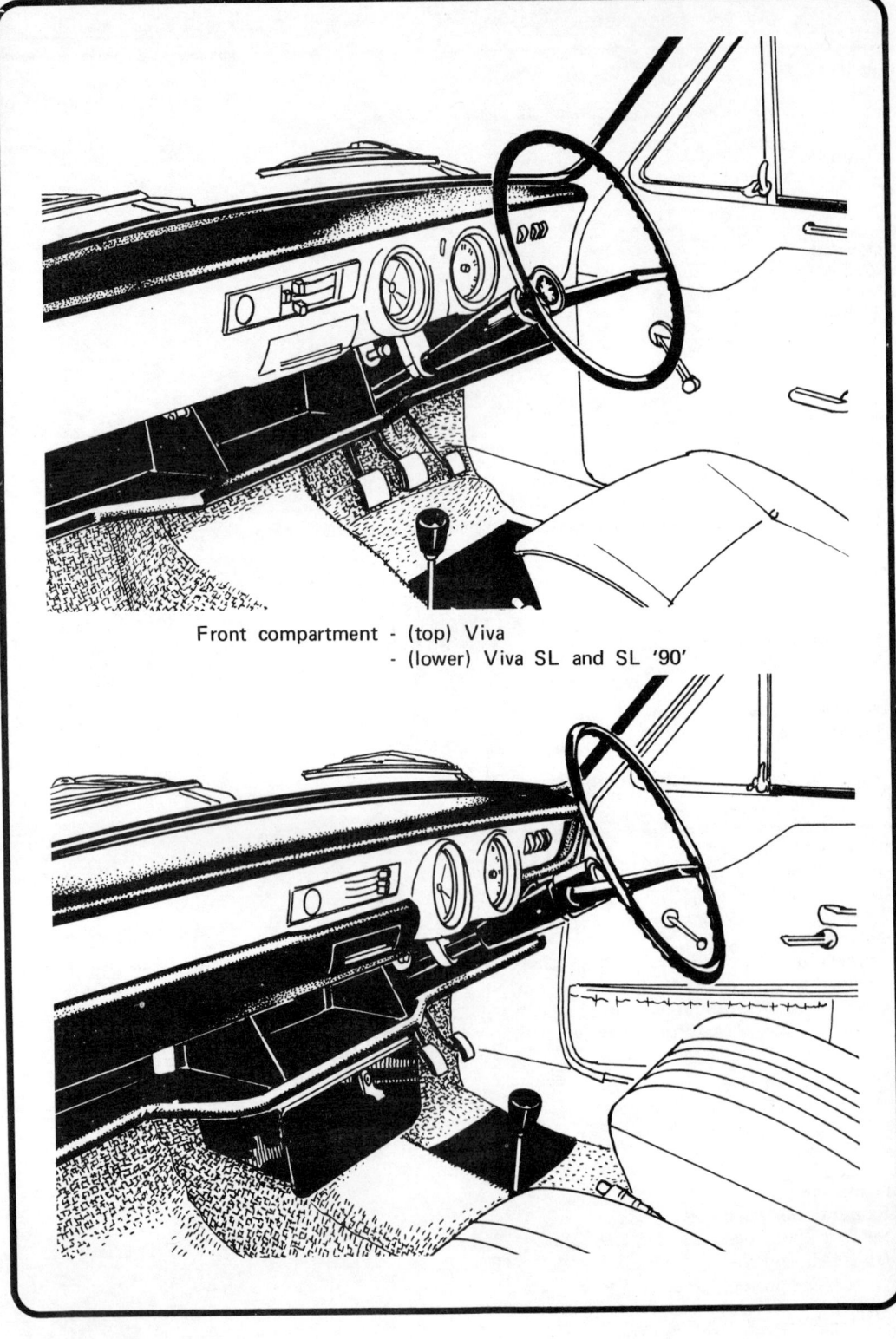

Front compartment - (top) Viva
- (lower) Viva SL and SL '90'

Brakes

All models except the 90 versions have hydraulically operated drum brakes with two leading shoes on the front drums and one leading and one trailing shoe on the rear drums.

90 models have disc brakes fitted at the front and servo power assistance to the whole hydraulic system. A handbrake operates the rear drums undependently using steel cables.

Battery

Voltage	12 v Positive (early models) or negative earth
Capacity	32 amp hour at 20 hour rate

Light bulbs

Head (rhd) (early models)	60/45 watt sealed beam
Head (rhd) (later models)	45/40 watt pre-focus
Head (lhd	50/40 or 45/40 pre-focus
Parking and front flasher)	
Tail stop)	6/21 watt small bayonet cap
Rear flasher	21 w single centre contact
Rear number plate	6 w miniature centre contact
Interior light	10 w festoon
Flasher warning)	
Instruments and warning lamps)	2.2 w miniature centre contact

Capacities

Petrol tank	7 gals	31.8 litres
Cooling system	10¼ pints	5.82 litres
Cooling system (with heater)	11¼ pints	6.39 litres
Engine sump (dry engine)	5½ pints	3.13 litres
Sump refill	4½ pints	2.55 litres
Sump refill incl filter change	5 pints	2.84 litres
Gearbox	1 pint	.57 litres
Rear axle	1¼ pints	.71 litres

Dimensions and Weights

Wheelbase	91.5 inch	(2.32 m)
Track (front)	47.4 inch	(1.20 m)
Track (rear)	48.2 inch	(1.22 m)
Overall length	155.1 (van 150.2)	(3.94 and 3.82 m)
Overall width	59.4 inch	(1.51 m)
Overall height	53.3 (van 59.5)	(1.35 and 1.51 m)
Ground clearance	4.7 inch	(127 m)

Kerb weight

Viva Saloon	1564 lb	(709 kg)
Viva De Luxe Saloon	1585 lb	(719 kg)
Viva SL Saloon	1612 lb	(731 kg)
Viva De Luxe 90	1601 lb	(727 kg)
Viva SL 90	1631 lb	(740 kg)
Van 6 cwt	1540 lb	(698 kg)
Van 8 cwt	1575 lb	(715 kg)
Beagle	1680 lb	(760 kg)

Road test data

	Standard Saloon	SL90
Maximum speed (mph)	76	84
Cruising speed (mph)	68	75
Cruising range (miles)	283	245
Maximum speed in gears: 3rd	68	69
2nd	43	44
1st	24	25
Acceleration through gears (seconds)		
0—30 mph	5.3	5.2
0—40 mph	8.6	8.4
0—50 mph	13.7	13.0
0—60 mph	22.1	19.7
0—70 mph	36.2	32.6
Standing ¼ mile (seconds)	21.5	21.3
Average fuel consumption (mpg)	39	35
Consumption at 50 mph (mpg)	40	39

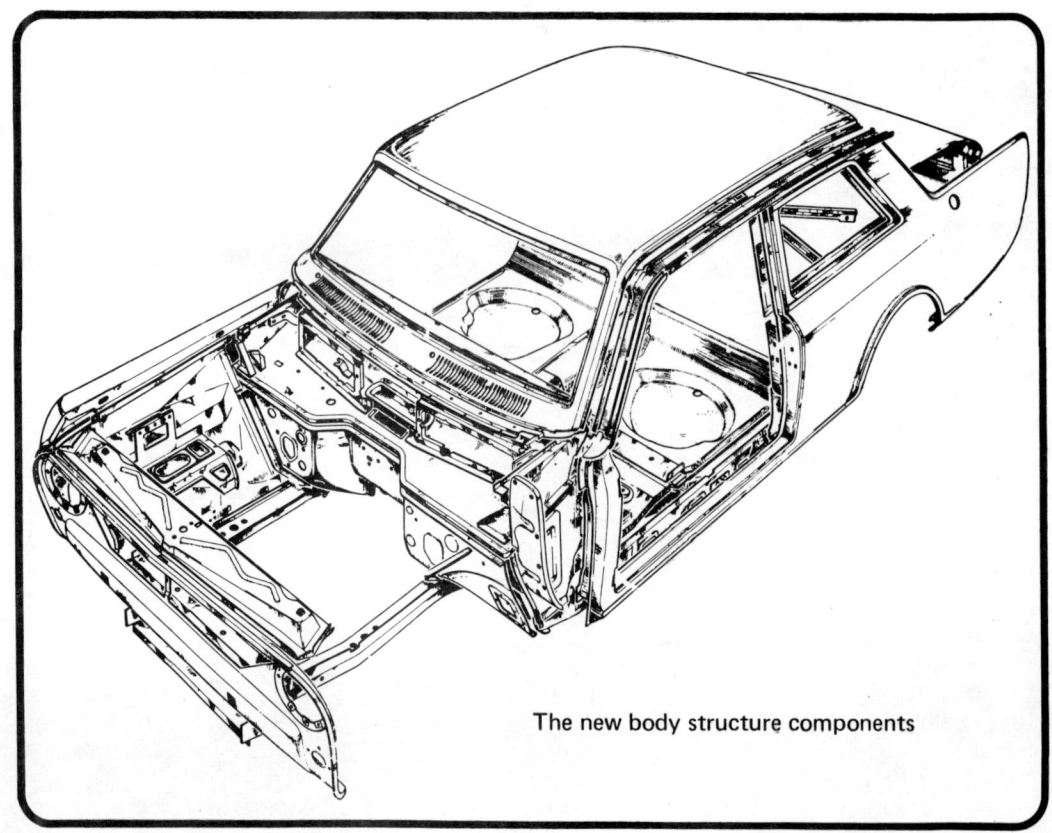

The new body structure components

Spares and Touring Pack

Before undertaking any long journey, whether in this country or abroad, it is advisable to thoroughly check your car and its contents. It is better to have the car serviced early, before the exact required time if necessary, rather than put it off until your return. Breakdown services, accredited dealers and spare part availability for your Viva HA are not always there when you need them, particularly abroad and in outlying districts of Great Britain.

There are two lists below, one giving spares which should **always** be carried in the car, and the other suggesting those which it is advisable to carry if undertaking a journey abroad. Some dealers are able to supply manufacturers' recommended touring packs on an hire/buy-if-you-use basis.

Always carry
First aid box and manual
Spare set of keys
Gallon can of petrol with filler spout (full)
List of car main agents
Breakdown triangle (compulsory on the continent)
Torch (with red flashing dome)
Fan belt
Finilec puncture sealer
Roll of PVC insulation tape
Temporary plastic windscreen
Length of electrical cable (heavy duty lighting circuit)
Screwdriver (medium sized)
Electrical screwdriver
Pair of pliers
Adjustable spanner (parrot jaw)
Distributor - rotor arm
             - condenser
             - set of points
1 tin of hand cleaner (Swarfega)

Going abroad
The articles in the 'Always Carry' list
Tow rope
Set of light bulbs
Set of spark plugs correctly gapped
Spare inner tube valves
Set of radiator hoses
Radiator sealer such as Holts Radweld
Set of fuses
Length of HT lead
Fire extinguisher
Tube of gasket jointing cement
Tin of Castrol Girling Brake Fluid
1 quart tin of Castrol GTX
1 spare head gasket set
As many other tools as you feel you may need
Adequate set of maps
List of Vauxhall/GM agents

Always keep this handbook in the car and produce it if you break down abroad. Non English speaking mechanics will find valuable information about your 'strange' car in it. There are many mechanical terms common to different languages - you can always point at the photographs, it may help!

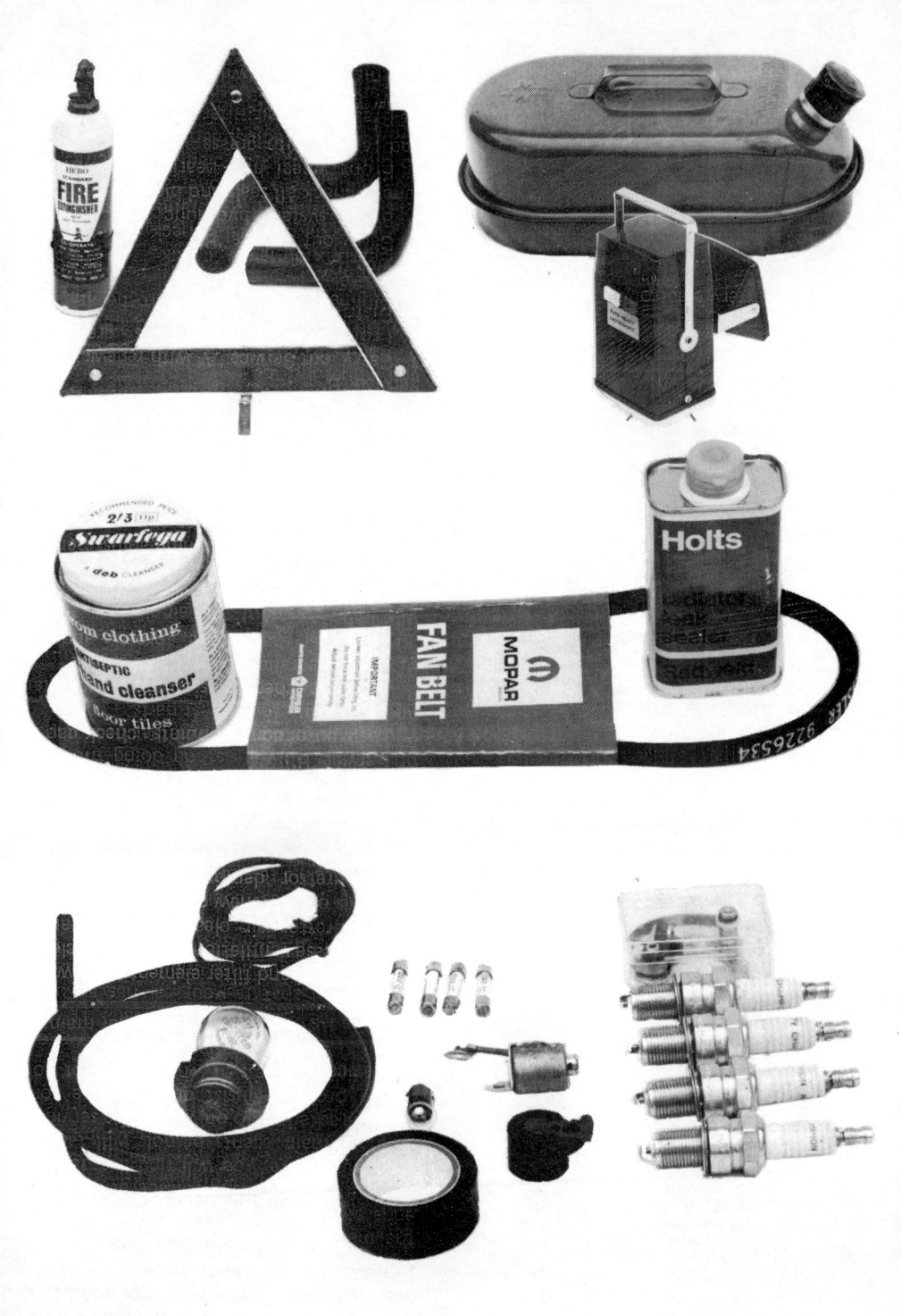

Tools

Routine Maintenance work requires a variety of tools to be carried out successfully. Most people have pliers and screwdrivers, but certain others will need to be acquired for special tasks. Buy good tools. Cheap ones do not last and can be dangerous. Sufficient tools are listed below to cover the maintenance tasks described.

Open ended spanners covering sizes:
   5/16 AF
   3/8 AF
   7/16 AF
   1/2 AF
   9/16 AF
1 Adjustable spanner - parrot jaw 10 inch
1 spark plug spanner
1 Pair pliers
1 Screwdriver - medium 8 inch
1 Screwdriver - crosshead 8 inch
1 Set feeler gauges
1 Brake adjusting spanner
1 File - small, fine
1 Oil can (Castrol Everyman)
1 Grease gun (Castrol LM)
Clean, non-fluffy cloth
Overalls
Hand cleanser (Swarfega)

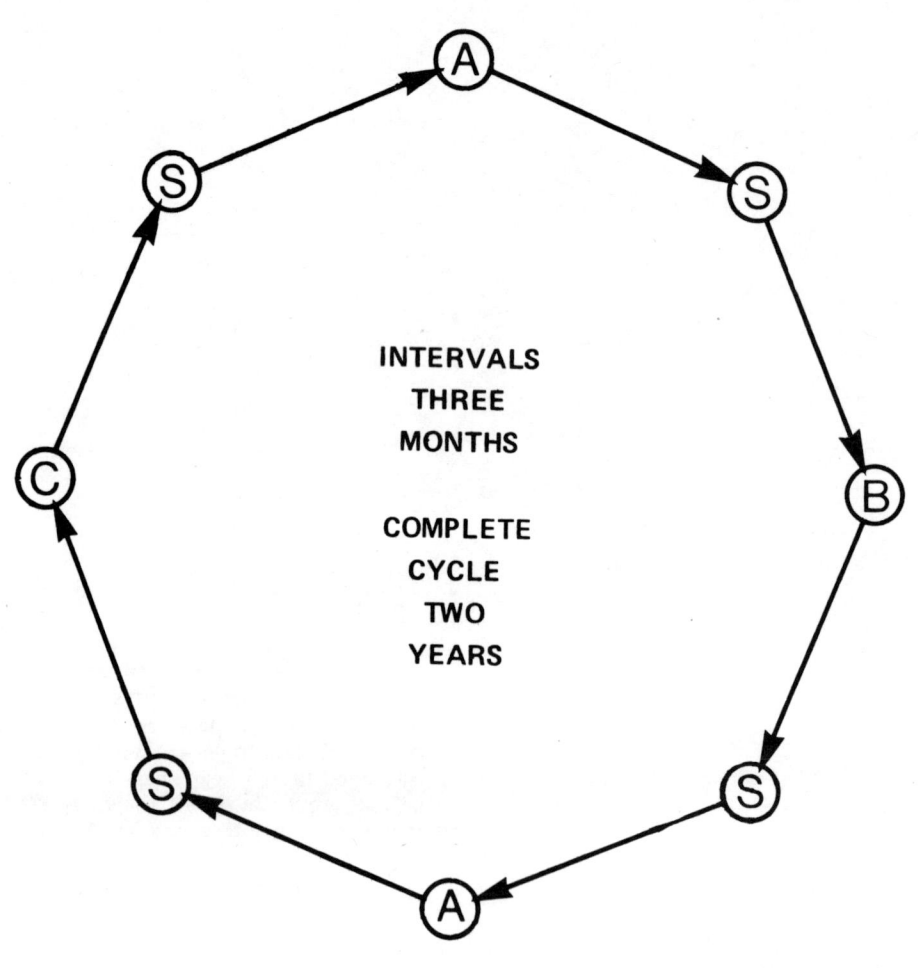

INTERVALS
THREE
MONTHS

COMPLETE
CYCLE
TWO
YEARS

Illustration of the servicing cycle which includes checks under the 'S' Service covering all safety requirements for the MOT Test

Routine maintenance

Introduction

If your car is your hobby, maintenance is not very exciting but at least there is the satisfaction of knowing you are able to keep it in good shape without spending a lot of money.

For those who regard a car as a necessity only, maintenance is a chore or an expense which involves either disrupting your routine use of the car, or occupying time which you feel could be otherwise better spent.

Whichever sort of motorist you are, one thing is common to all - the maintenance must be done. If it is ignored, delayed, or forgotten, then your routine use will be disrupted even more inconveniently, or your time and expense will be greatly increased.

The manufacturer's recommendations under their 'Euroservice 365 Maintenance Plan' provide for a service frequency based on a time interval. This time interval uses a basis of an annual average mileage of 12000. The intension is to ensure a service or safety check every three months, at least, regardless of distance travelled. Mileages in excess of the average will normally be on vehicles used for business, or by fleet operators. For the private motorist excess mileage - if consistent - may justify a greater service frequency. This will be left to the discretion of the owner. The 'safety check' which is part of the maintenance plan, shows that the manufacturers acknowledge that even though nothing may need **doing**, everything needs **checking** at regular intervals.

The need for certain maintenance tasks unconnected with safety is often dictated by varying circumstances. Rather than just being vague, such tasks have been included at specified intervals in the standard schedules. In this way they may be purposely omitted but cannot be forgotten.

To keep a record of maintenance carried out is the easiest way of making sure that all the checks and operations are dealt with at the correct time. Such a record will be advantageous when the car is sold or traded-in. (No record in itself, is absolute proof that work has been carried out as stated. It is unlikely though that a continuous record of fictitious information would be kept!).

WHAT IS TO BE DONE AND WHEN

Your car falls into one of the following categories:

1 Yours since new
2 Secondhand with an up-to-date maintenance record
3 Secondhand with no maintenance record

If no service record is available when acquiring the car start the service cycle on Service 'C' together with an 'S' Safety Check.

WEEKLY

Most easily done when buying petrol. Check:
Radiator coolant level
Engine oil level
Battery electrolyte level
Tyre pressures

A good garage should do these checks for you without question or charge, if asked, when petrol is bought. You should only pay for any oil required.

Inspection Service 'S' Safety Check. Incorporates MOT Test Checks.

1 Brake master cylinder fluid level
2 Front wheel hub bearing adjustment
3 Steering linkage and ball joint condition
4 Brake linings and pads - adjustment and wear
5 Brake hydraulic fluid pipe condition
6 Brake hydraulic wheel cylinder condition
7 Suspension - Springs
8 Exhaust system - tightness and leaks
9 Lamps and indicators - bulbs and beam alignment
10 Windscreen wipers
11 Handbrake lever setting
12 Tyre condition
13 Seat belts and anchorages

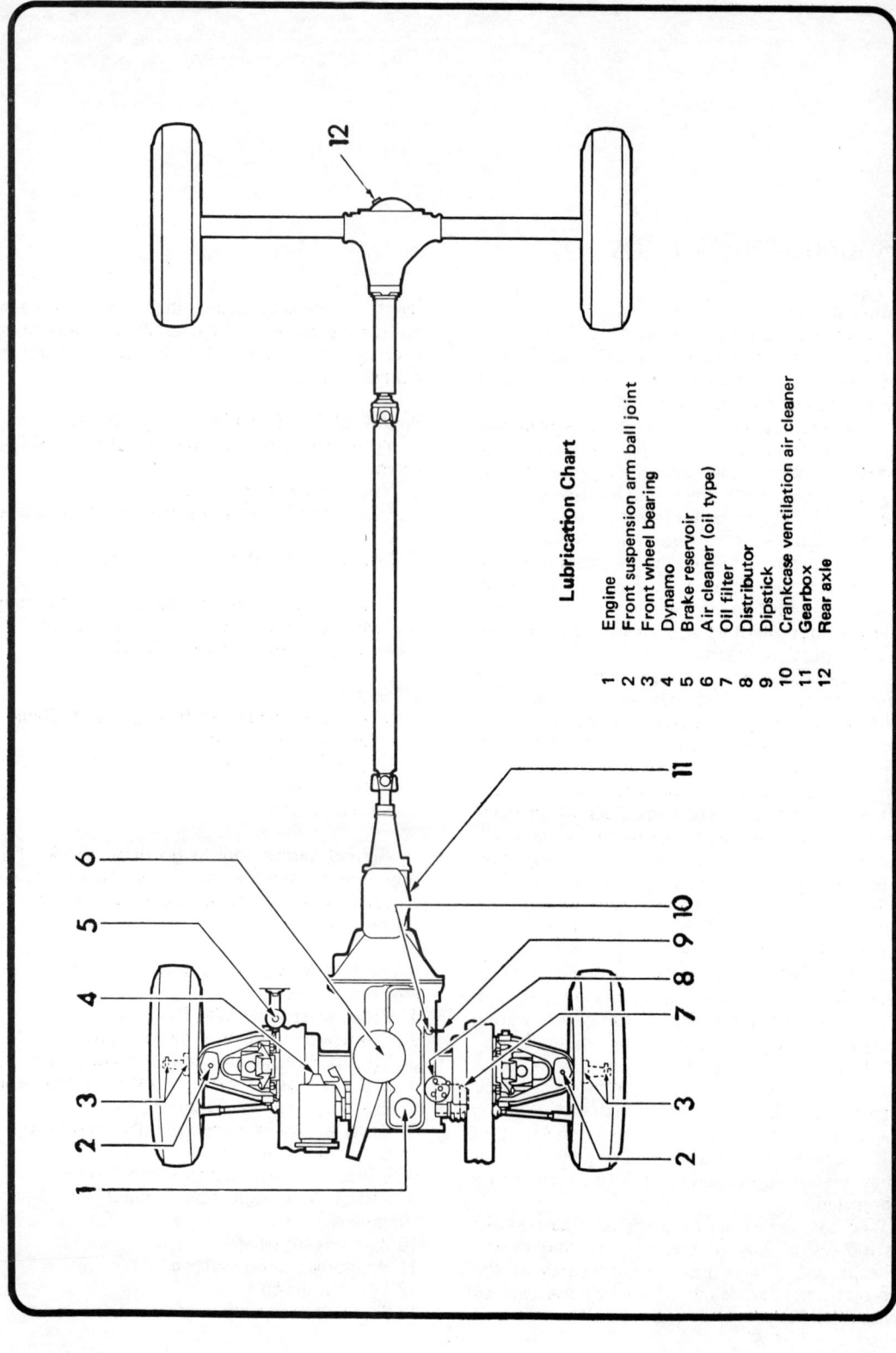

Lubrication Chart

1 Engine
2 Front suspension arm ball joint
3 Front wheel bearing
4 Dynamo
5 Brake reservoir
6 Air cleaner (oil type)
7 Oil filter
8 Distributor
9 Dipstick
10 Crankcase ventilation air cleaner
11 Gearbox
12 Rear axle

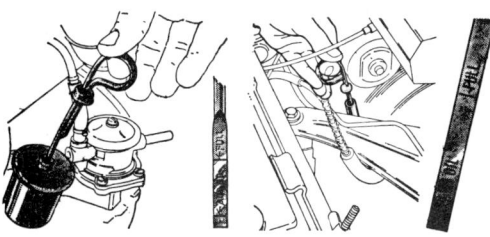

Dipstick reading

Battery electrolyte

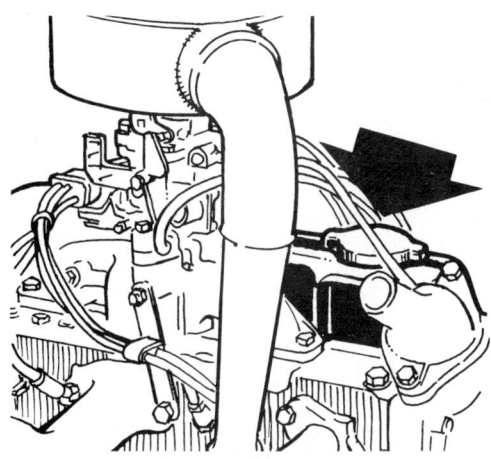

Engine oil top up

Service 'A'

1 Engine oil and filter element - renew
2 Crankcase ventilation air cleaner - clean
3 Carburettor air cleaner - tap clean (paper elements only. Renew on Service 'B').
4 Carburettor damper '90' engines - check damper oil
5 Fuel pump - clean filter gauze (renew on Service 'B')
6 Spark plugs - remove, clean and reset (renew on Service 'B')
7 Distributor contact points - check gap setting and adjust
8 Fan belt - check tension and adjust
9 Valve clearances - check and adjust
10 Linkages - handbrake, throttle and clutch - lubricate
11 Gearbox oil level - check
12 Rear axle oil level - check
13 Carburettor slow running adjustment
14 Timing chain tensioner adjustment
15 Clutch pedal free play adjustment
16 Brake shoe adjustment and lining wear
17 Brake servo air filter (disc brakes) - renew
18 Generator rear bush - lubricate

Service 'B'

1 Carry out Service 'A' with renewals as stated
2 Front suspension ball joints - grease
3 Distributor - lubricate

Service 'C'

1 Carry out Service 'B'
2 Brake system hydraulic fluid - drain out, renew, check all seals and bleed system
3 Front wheel hub bearings - removal, clean and repack with grease

HOW TO DO IT

This handbook will show you how to do all the service operations yourself. It must be emphasised that if your car has an unbroken record of maintenance undertaken since new by an authorised Vauxhall dealer and is in excellent condition overall, it may be unwise to interrupt the maintenance record established. The existence of such a record as part of the value of the car must be taken into consideration.

Furthermore, you will find that few garages, whether main agents or not, will take kindly to being asked to do only part of a service. They would probably insist on doing the complete schedule regardless of whether or not you said you had done the easiest parts.

Also, just because the two year maintenance

cycle is religiously followed, one cannot expect the car to last forever. The manufacturers do not publicise the expected life of the car or of its main components. Broadly speaking one may have to face parts replacements on the engine, gearbox, front suspension, steering and back axle after three maintenance cycles have elapsed. If the maintenance has been irregular, the renewals will be needed earlier. Records of overhauls and renewals of components are therefore particularly valuable and greatly affect the re-sale value if they are properly documented and can be proven.

WEEKLY

Radiator coolant level check

Wait until the engine is cool. Raise the bonnet and prop it open. If the engine is very hot and you wish to remove the cap, use a good sized wad of cloth over it as there may be a considerable pressure of steam behind it which could scald you.

Turn the cap anticlockwise and if the engine is hot and you are using a cloth, keep it pressed down. Release it slowly until all the pressure has escaped. Lift the cap out.

The level of the coolant in the radiator should be 1 inch/25 mm below the **bottom** of the filler neck. Do not overfill or it will tend to siphon out from the overflow pipe. If the radiator has been filled with an antifreeze mixture it is important to top up the level with a mixture of the same strength. Otherwise, if only water is added, the coolant will be diluted and therefore get less and less effective the more the topping up is done. If topping up is required after each journey and is quantity, (over 1 pint per week) there is likely to be something wrong and it should be investigated.

Oil - engine sump level check

If the car has been running, wait five minutes for the oil to drain back down to the sump. The car should be standing level. Remove the level dipstick, wipe it clean and replace it fully home. Remove it and note the level mark of the oil. Under no circumstances should it be below the 'add oil' mark. The quantity needed to raise it from the 'add oil' to 'full' mark is 2 pints. Do not add oil over the 'full' mark as it will be wasted.

If it is necessary to add oil every week, or more often, and your mileage is no more than average (250 miles) then this is an indication of

Tyre pressure check

Brake master cylinder fluid top-up

Front wheel hub adjustment

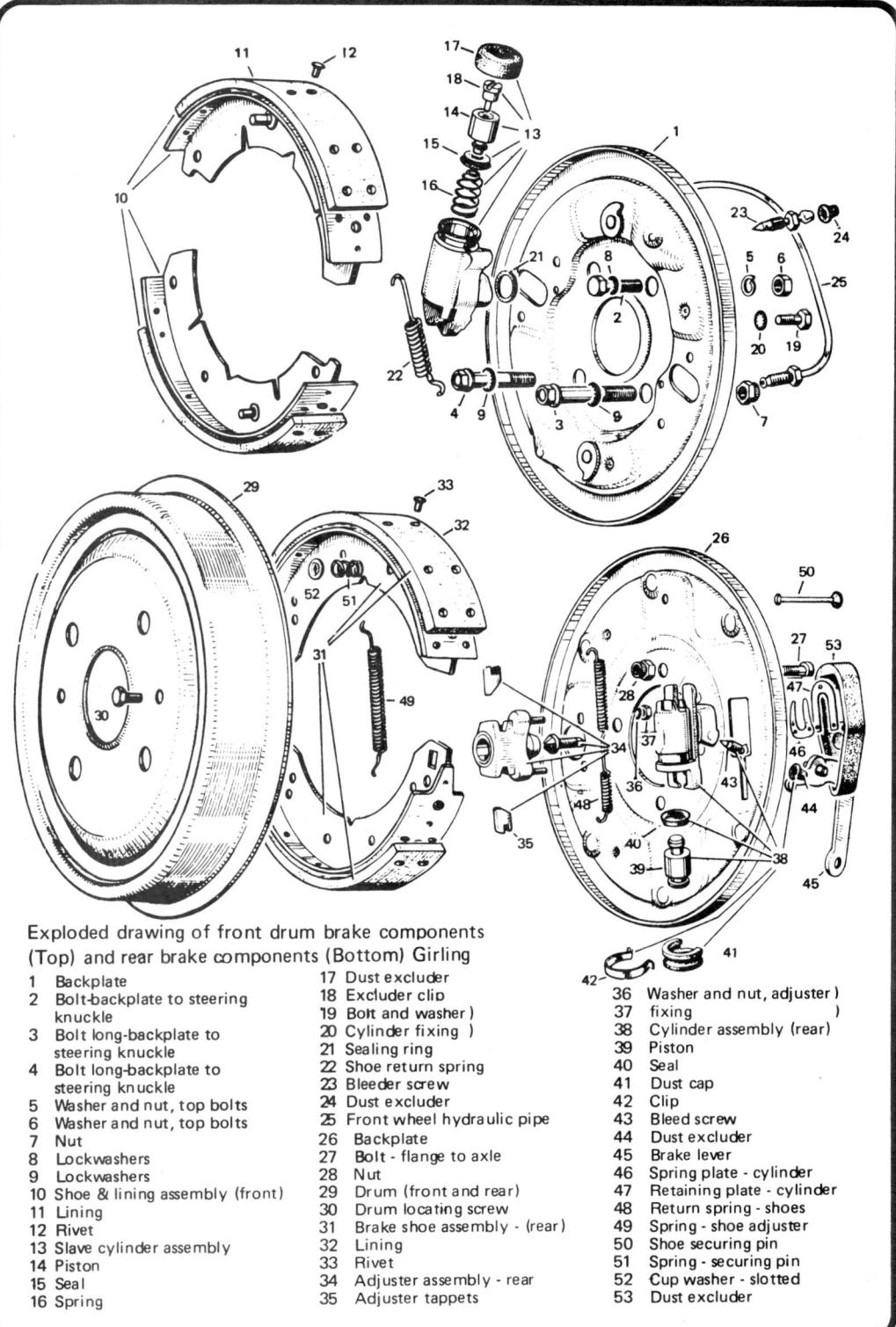

Exploded drawing of front drum brake components
(Top) and rear brake components (Bottom) Girling

1	Backplate	17	Dust excluder	36	Washer and nut, adjuster)
2	Bolt-backplate to steering knuckle	18	Excluder clip	37	fixing)
		19	Bolt and washer)	38	Cylinder assembly (rear)
3	Bolt long-backplate to steering knuckle	20	Cylinder fixing)	39	Piston
		21	Sealing ring	40	Seal
4	Bolt long-backplate to steering knuckle	22	Shoe return spring	41	Dust cap
		23	Bleeder screw	42	Clip
5	Washer and nut, top bolts	24	Dust excluder	43	Bleed screw
6	Washer and nut, top bolts	25	Front wheel hydraulic pipe	44	Dust excluder
7	Nut	26	Backplate	45	Brake lever
8	Lockwashers	27	Bolt - flange to axle	46	Spring plate - cylinder
9	Lockwashers	28	Nut	47	Retaining plate - cylinder
10	Shoe & lining assembly (front)	29	Drum (front and rear)	48	Return spring - shoes
11	Lining	30	Drum locating screw	49	Spring - shoe adjuster
12	Rivet	31	Brake shoe assembly - (rear)	50	Shoe securing pin
13	Slave cylinder assembly	32	Lining	51	Spring - securing pin
14	Piston	33	Rivet	52	Cup washer - slotted
15	Seal	34	Adjuster assembly - rear	53	Dust excluder
16	Spring	35	Adjuster tappets		

engine wear. Do not buy cheap oil. You will save nothing in the long run. A good quality multigrade with anti-corrosion additives such as Castrol GTX is recommended.

Battery - checking electrolyte level

One of the best ways of getting maximum life from the battery is regular checking and topping up of the electrolyte. It is often ignored or overlooked.

Depending on the type of battery fitted the method of topping up will vary. For patented automatic level types follow the instructions. The requirement is the same for all, however, to ensure that the electrolyte liquid just covers the separator plates (or the guard above them). Add distilled water from a suitably nozzled container until this is achieved. Do not overfill each cell as this will dilute the electrolyte and the operation of the battery will be less efficient over a period of time. As a battery gets older, the need for topping up will increase. Provided the battery still performs satisfactorily this is nothing to worry about. Little and often is the rule for topping up.

Always keep the top of the battery perfectly clean and dry.

Tyre pressures

Correct tyre pressures are essential for ensuring proper behaviour of the car when steering and braking.

If any tyre shows signs of losing pressure more significantly than the rest, investigate it for it must have a leak.

Do not check or adjust pressures when the tyres are hot from a fast run on a hot day. If they obviously need air, recheck the pressures when they are cool.

SERVICE 'S' SAFETY CHECK (MOT)

Provided regular servicing is carried out the 'S' check should result in one or two minor adjustments at most. When a car has passed through two or more complete maintenance cycles it may be assumed that certain parts checked will need renewal. None of the work carried out on Service 'A' has any connection with the checks in Service 'S'.

1 Brake master cylinder fluid level

Carefully clean the top of the fluid reservoir round the cap and then remove the cap. The fluid level should be ¼ inch/6 mm below the edge of the rim. It should be topped up with

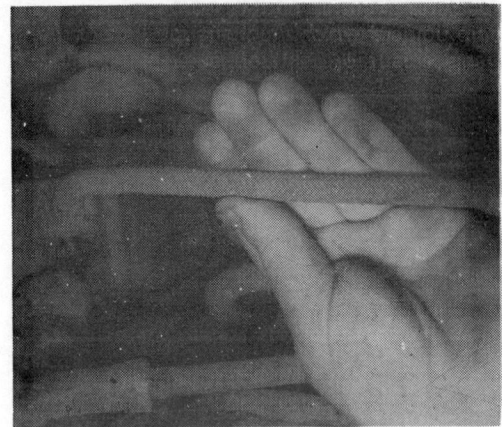
Flexible hydraulic pipe check

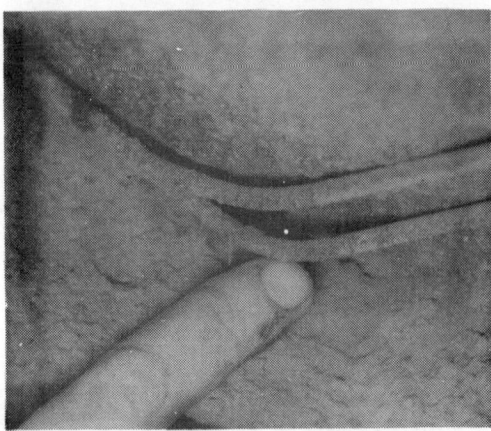
Rigid hydraulic pipe check

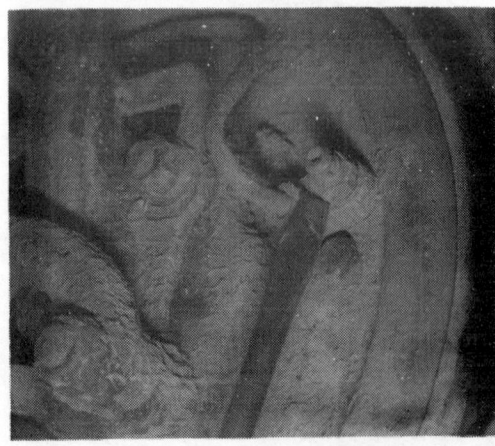
Back plate and bleed nipple check

Removal of the drum holding screw

Removal of front drum and drum/lining inspection

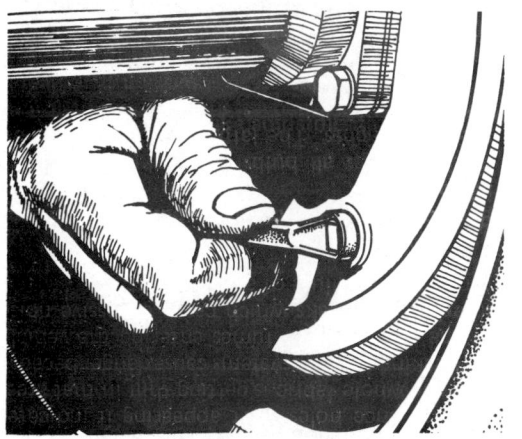

Rear brake adjustment

Castrol Girling Crimson Brake Fluid. Under normal conditions the level should not drop significantly (more than ¼ inch below the correct limit). If it is noticeably lower than this it should be checked again - after topping up - within a week. Any continued sign of a level drop indicates a fault and this will need careful investigation.

2 Front wheel hub bearing adjustment

The ball bearings on which the front wheels revolve wear fractionally as time passes and, as a result, the wheel/hub can be a little slack. If this is left unadjusted the wear will accelerate and serious slackness will affect the steering of the car.

Jack up the front of the car so that the wheel is clear of the ground and free to revolve.

Grip the tyre, one hand at the top and the other at the bottom and try to rock the wheel. Very little force is needed. If the bearing is slack it will be possible to feel the wheel rocking. The degree of slackness can vary but in any case it is best to have it attended to. If you are experiencing severe tyre wear and/or imprecise steering, the bearing is possibly very slack and should be attended to with urgency.

To adjust the wheel bearing remove the hub cap. Then remove the domed dust cover which covers the bearing in the centre of the wheel. This cover is a tight push fit and can be taken out with a few taps from side to side to gradually work it out. The large nut with a split pin will then be visible. Before removing the split pin make sure you have a new one available because it cannot be re-used.

Remove the split pin. Using a tubular spanner slacken the nut about half a turn and then spin the wheel and tighten the nut. Use the spanner without a tommy bar. If you overtighten the nut, the wheel will not spin freely. If you are unable to eliminate the play in the bearing without causing the bearing to bind, or if it feels rough, it must be worn out and should be renewed.

When adjustment is correct the nut may be loosened a fraction so that the split pin hole in the stub axle lines up with two of the slots. Do not overtighten the nut to achieve this. Always fit a new split pin.

3 Brake hydraulic fluid pipe condition

Any leak in the hydraulic system renders all brakes ineffective. A metal pipe leads fluid to each wheel, and a flexible pipe is used where movement of each front wheel and of the back axle requires it. The metal pipes can, and do, corrode away from the outside in time and must be replaced before they corrode right through.

Underneath the car the pipes are clipped to the bodywork. They should be traced and cleaned free of road dirt throughout their length along the bodyframe and top of the back axle casing. Use a wire brush to clear them. Any signs of pitting or other damage will be clearly seen. Pitted sections must be taken out and renewed without delay. If you are in an area which uses salt on the roads in winter the dangers of corrosion are increased.

The flexible hose should be twisted about a little and examined for cracks. Any signs of deterioration will mean that renewal of the hose is necessary.

If during examination of the pipes any sign of fluid leakage is seen, the car must not be used until a thorough investigation and repair has been carried out.

4 Brake hydraulic wheel cylinder condition

This check is done at the same time as examination of the fluid pipes. It mainly consists of examining the backplate of each brake where signs of fluid leakage would show if the wheel cylinder seals leak. In view of the fact that both oil or grease could conceivably work its way on to the backplate it is essential that the difference is noticed. Hydraulic fluid has a distinctive smell (lift the reservoir cap to obtain an indication) and it should be possible to distinguish what is leaking. If in any doubt do not delay in having it checked by removing the brake drum. On disc brake models any leak at the wheel cylinder will show at the bottom of the main body of the brake calliper.

Leaking cylinders are dangerous and must be repaired immediately.

5 Brake linings and pads - adjustment and wear

Expect to adjust drum brakes (disc brakes are self-adjusting) every three months at least. The need is indicated when the pedal has to move a long way before the brakes operate.

If you are doing an adjustment for the first time it is best to remove the wheel first as the adjusting screws are somewhat inaccessible. Jack up the car and remove the wheel. For front drum brakes there are two adjusting screws,

one at the top and bottom of the brake back-plate. The head of the screw is square and quite small. A proper key spanner should be used to turn it. Anything else is likely to burr the edges making it progressively more difficult to turn. Often the adjusting screws are stiff due to road dirt and rust. If therefore you have difficulty in moving them, clean them off thoroughly and apply a quantity of penetrating oil. Leave them for some time.

To adjust the brake shoes, turn the adjuster clockwise until it is impossible to turn the brake drum. Then turn it back one or two notches until the drum is free to rotate once more. Repeat this procedure for the other adjuster.

Rear brakes have a single adjuster only at the top of the backplate. Adjustment is the same as for the front brakes.

If brakes are left in need of adjustment for too long a time, it is likely that after adjustment they will not work quite as sharply as they did before, even though they start to operate much sooner. This condition will improve after some use but it may call for further adjustment later. Expect drum brake linings to last approximately twelve months before renewal is required, depending on how you drive and where you drive. Disc pads, whilst needing no actual adjustment, may be examined without difficulty. Remove the wheel and look down into the calliper aperture. The pad consists of a metal backing plate to which friction material is bonded. The friction material should not be less then 1/8 inch (3.2 mm) in thickness. If it is, new pads are needed. Brakes are tested by MOT testing stations using a decelerometer. A good indication of properly working brakes can be obtained by standing an ordinary house brick on its long narrow side at right angles to the direction of travel on the front passenger floor. Firm (not crash) application of the brakes should cause the brick to topple over immediately without any wheels locking. Hand-brake application at the same speed should cause it to teeter at least and it should just topple over.

6 Steering linkage and ball joint condition

This check involves jacking up each of the front wheels in turn and should be done when other tests requiring jacking are done.

With the car jacked up and the wheel clear of the ground, grip the tyre with a hand at each side. Try and rock it sideways. Do not apply sustained pressure in any direction but try and

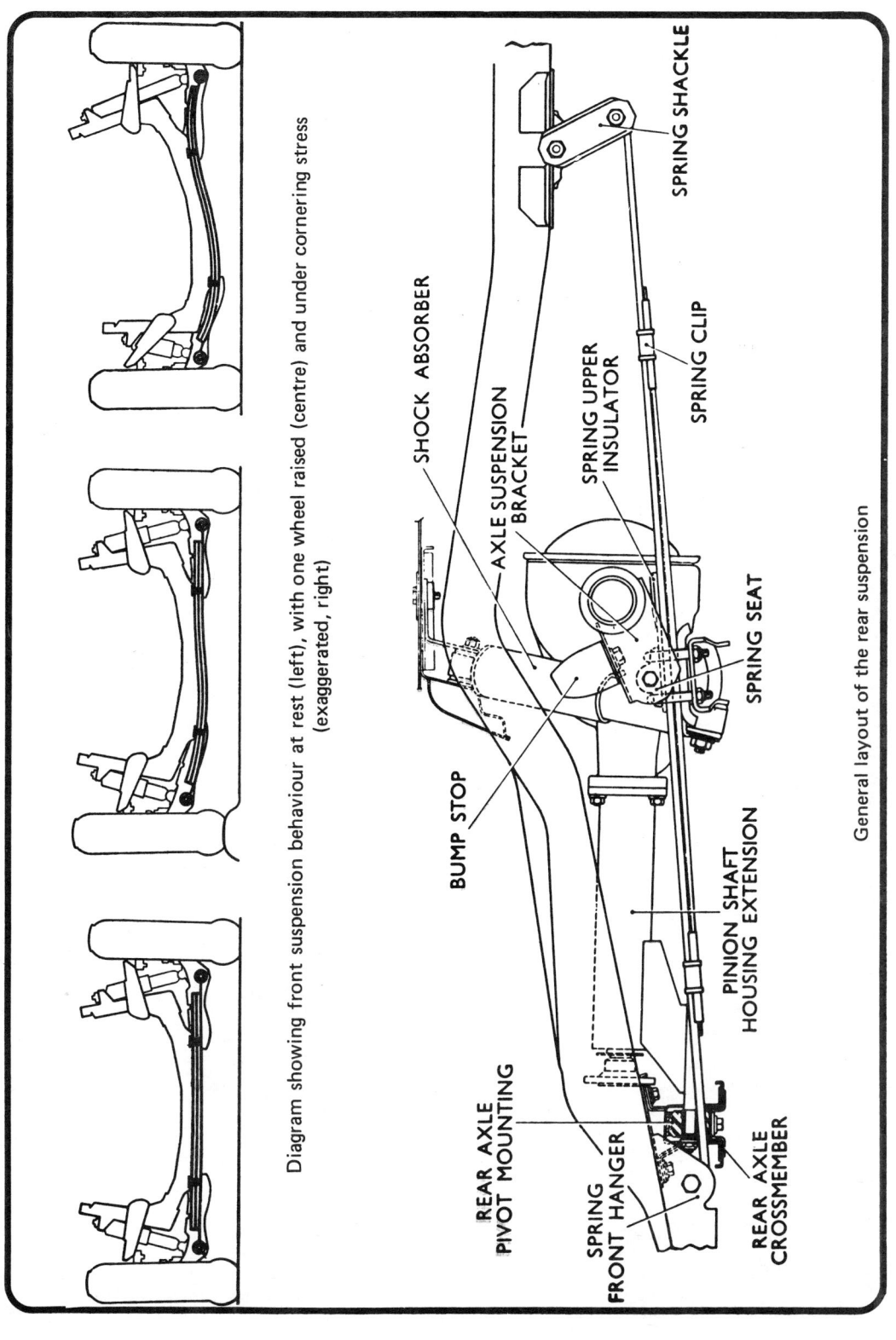

Diagram showing front suspension behaviour at rest (left), with one wheel raised (centre) and under cornering stress (exaggerated, right)

SHOCK ABSORBER

SPRING SHACKLE

AXLE SUSPENSION
BRACKET

SPRING UPPER
INSULATOR

SPRING CLIP

BUMP STOP

SPRING SEAT

REAR AXLE
PIVOT MOUNTING

PINION SHAFT
HOUSING EXTENSION

SPRING
FRONT HANGER

REAR AXLE
CROSSMEMBER

General layout of the rear suspension

move it back and forth. If the wheel can move without the steering wheel turning then there must be some wear in the linkage between the two. Look at the short track rod between the steering arm on the wheel and the steering gear rack, and rock the wheel again. Notice where the play is occurring. It will probably be at the wheel end of the rod in the ball joint. Such a condition requires renewal of the joint. Repeat the check on the other front wheel. If the play does not come from any of the track rod joints the fault must lie in the steering gear, which is more serious. This requires competent garage attention and could be expensive.

7 Suspension - springs and shock absorbers

Stand the car on level ground. If one corner appears low it could be due to a weak or broken spring. It will be obvious on examination if any of the springs are broken. In either case the faulty spring should be renewed.

The double acting telescopic shock absorbers are sealed. If any one of them shows any indication of oil leakage it must be renewed. The upper and lower mounting bushes should be examined for signs of looseness too. To check the operation of a shock absorber the car may be 'bounced' by pressing it down at each corner in turn. The vehicle should rebound and stop. If it continues to bounce up and down it is a fair indication that the shock absorber is not functioning properly and should be renewed.

8 Exhaust system - tightness and leaks

If there are any holes in the exhaust system they can usually be heard and must be attended to without delay. The brackets and hangers which support the system under the car must be intact. If they are not, a strain will be imposed on the exhaust system which could then fracture. Temporary repairs to small leaks can be made with one of the proprietary sealers or 'bandages' in the Holts range. These should however be regarded as short term operations because once holes start appearing it indicates that the whole fabric is getting thin in that area.

Leaking exhaust systems cause danger because of the possibility of fumes entering the vehicle interior. Bad leaks which cause excessive noise can result in failure of an MOT test.

9 Lamps and indicators - bulbs and beam alignment

Check that all bulbs are working, including the brake lights. The latter can be checked by

Front suspension assembly - cutaway at the lower wishbone fulcrum pin and bushes

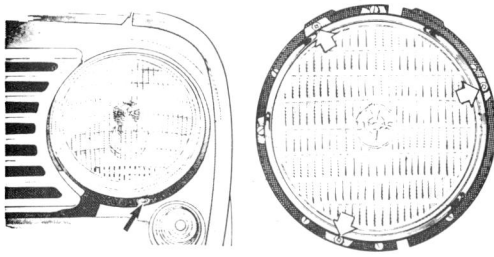

Headlamp fixture screws

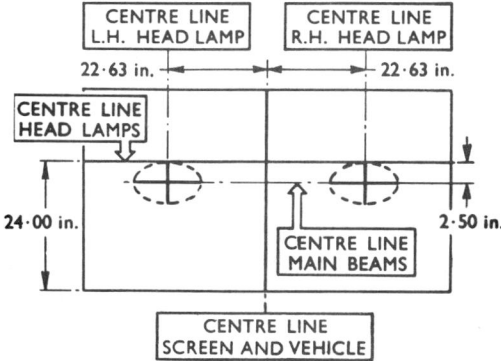

Diagram of correct headlamp beam setting

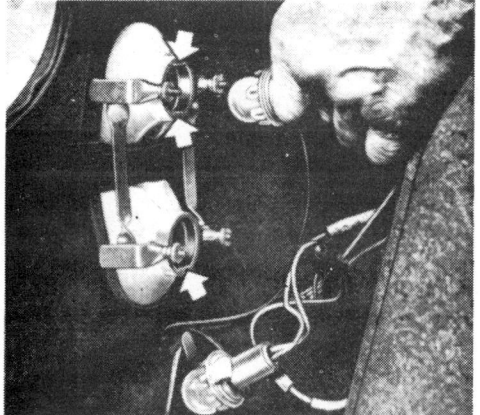

Replacement of tail/stop and flasher lamp bulb holders. Arrows indicate the flats in the apertures to ensure correct lamp locations.

operating the brake pedal when the ignition is switched on.

Headlamp bulbs are replaceable and access to them is by first removing the screw securing the moulding around the headlamp. Then undo the three cross head screws holding the lamp unit. Do not confuse these with the beam alignment adjusting screws. Lift the lamp out. Pull off the connection block. When the clips holding the bulb into the lamp reflector are released the bulb may be removed. When fitting a new one see that the flange on the bulb engages the slot in the body. The front side light bulbs are also housed in the headlamp reflector except on very early models. These are reached by pulling the claw type bulb holder from the headlamp body.

The front turn indicator bulbs are housed in the amber lenses mounted on the wing below the front bumper. Remove the two screws holding the lens in position and pull it off. After having fitted the new bulb make sure that both the lens gasket and the lens are fitting snugly before tightening the screws. If they should be out of position there is a possibility of the lens cracking. Do not overtighten the screws.

The stop, tail and turn signal lamps at the rear are incorporated in a single housing and access to the bulbs is from inside the boot. Remove the cover and pull out the snap fit bulb holder and bulb as required. The stop/tail lamp bulb has an offset bayonet pin fitting. Make sure that the double filaments are connected the proper way round. On SL models the two lights at the rear are in separate lens housings and each bulb is accessible after undoing the two screws holding the lens in position.

The rear number plate light bulbs can be removed when the screws holding the hooded lenses to the rear bumper are removed.

The headlamp beam alignment is something which rarely alters and is best set using proper optical alignment equipment. Lamps which do not dip correctly are illegal and if it is obvious that yours need attention do not delay. If the lamps are seriously misaligned temporary adjustment can be made by turning the adjuster screws. To reach these, first remove the headlamp moulding and, with the vehicle facing a vertical wall at a distance of 25 feet, set the beams as indicated in the drawing.

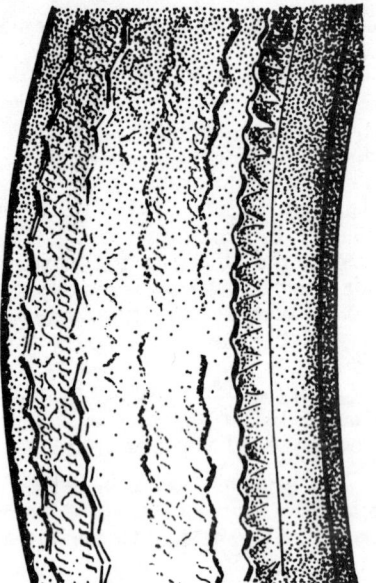

Incorrect tyre pressure

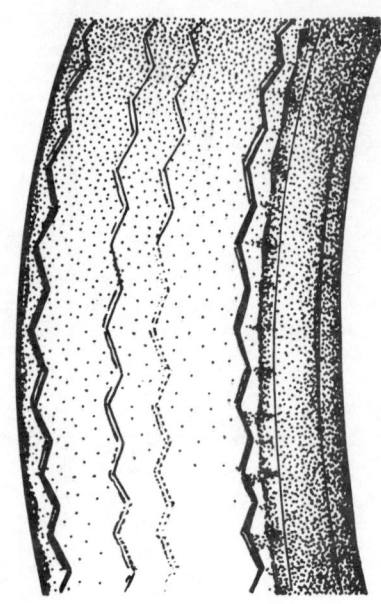

Uneven wear (out of balance or suspension fault)

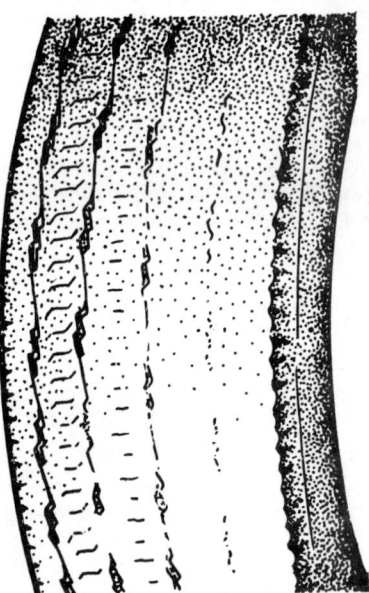

Excessive toe-in or toe-out

Illustrated on this page are three examples of very badly and irregularly worn tyres (now illegal). It is totally unnecessary for this type of wear to take place. It is possible to rectify the causes of these types of wear early on if regular checking takes place.

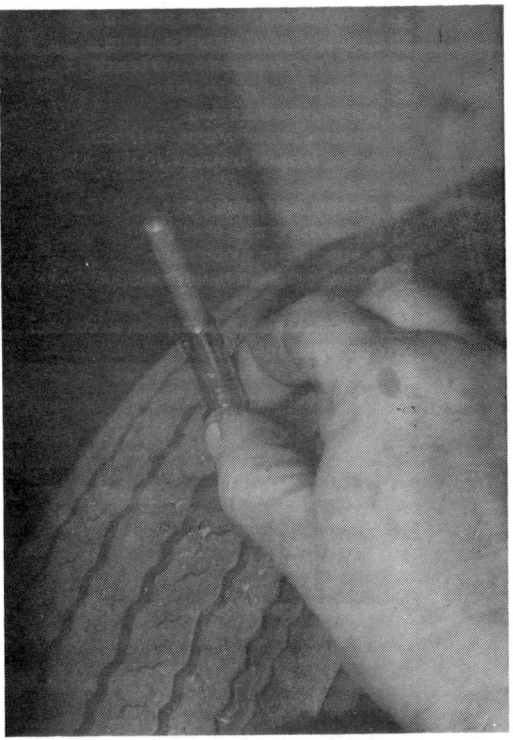

Tyre tread depth measurement

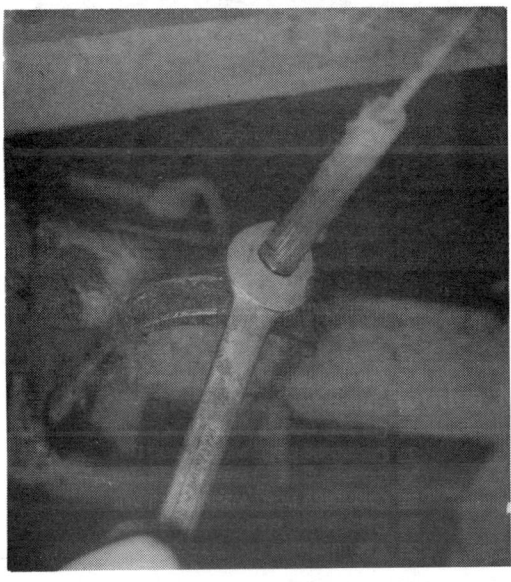

Handbrake adjustment

10 Windscreen wipers

If the windscreen wipers do not function the car will fail the MOT test. If they will work when 'helped' by pushing them after the motor is switched on then it usually means that the linkage is worn. This must be attended to otherwise the motor is likely to get overloaded and will burn out. This repair should be entrusted to your garage.

11 Handbrake lever setting and adjustment

Before assuming that the handbrake lever and cables are in need of adjustment the adjustment of the rear brake shoes should have been checked first as described under Item 16, Page 47. When this has been done the handbrake should be fully on when 5 or 6 clicks of the ratchet have been pulled on. If it has to travel further it means that the cable has stretched. Adjustment can be made by altering the setting of the screwed adjuster rod at the end of the single cable where it joins the yoke of the stretcher cable. Undo the locknut and rotate the adjuster as required.

12 Tyre condition

Tyres should have at least 1 mm depth of tread across their full contact width. They should also be free from cuts, ruptures and severe abrasions in their side walls.

Radial and cross-ply tyres should not be mixed on the same vehicle but if circumstances force it then two of the four must be radials, on the rear wheels only. Any other arrangement is both dangerous and illegal.

Tyres which are damaged or of the wrong mix as described will not be passed for the MOT test.

13 Seat belts and anchorages

Examine the full length of the seat belts particularly at loops and buckles where fraying may occur.

See that the bolts at the anchorage points are tight.

Have your garage recheck and replace any suspect parts of the seat belts and mounting points.

SERVICE 'A'

1 Engine oil and oil filter element - refill and renew

Run the engine until it reaches normal working temperature and then park the car on level ground. Obtain a container which will hold a minimum of 1 gallon and is shallow enough to position under the engine sump. Using the correct spanner, undo the large hexagonal plug in the sump and let the oil drain out.

Whilst the oil is draining out the oil filter element may be removed. At the front of the engine below the distributor on the left, the oil filter housing projects from the engine block. A fixing bolt runs through the centre. Unscrew the bolt and pull it out as far as it will go. When the housing is loose, oil will leak out, so be ready to hold it up and remove it from the car quickly before oil gets all over the place. If the housing sticks in position give it a smart tap with the hand to dislodge it.

Lift out the old element from inside the housing and throw it away. Do not try to take out the spring and plate round the centre bolt. They are meant to stay put. Flush out the interior of the casing thoroughly with paraffin to remove any sludge.

The circular groove in the engine block where the oil filter cover fits will have a sealing ring in it. Poke this out with a small screwdriver or point of a nail. Do not throw it away until you have made sure that the new sealing ring supplied with your new filter is the correct size. Some filters are supplied with two sealing rings - select the one which is the same as the one you have taken out.

Fit the new sealing ring in the groove in the block. This must be done with care to make sure it fits flat in the bottom of the groove. It must not twist over, or lie on edge, or it will leak.

Place the new filter element in the cover. It can go in either way round. If you have time it is a good idea to soak the element in clean oil (Castrol GTX) before fitting it. It reduces the first few seconds of starting up. Place the cover back into position and tighten up the bolt, revolving the cover finally to make sure it is seated on the sealing ring snugly.

By this time all the old oil should have drained out underneath. Remove the oil receptacle. Do not pour old oil down the drain. Most garages will accept this old oil - they have proper facilities for its disposal. If you decide to burn it make sure the smoke does not cause a nuisance and that you do not start an uncontrollable fire.

Check that the drain plug washer is intact. Replace and tighten the plug. If you need a new

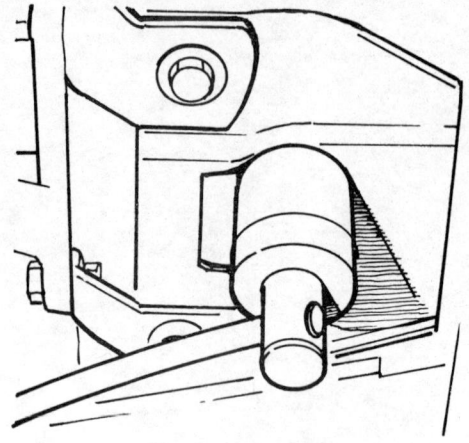

Sump drain plug

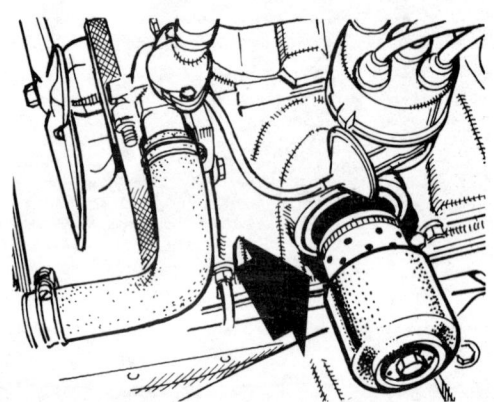

Oil filter

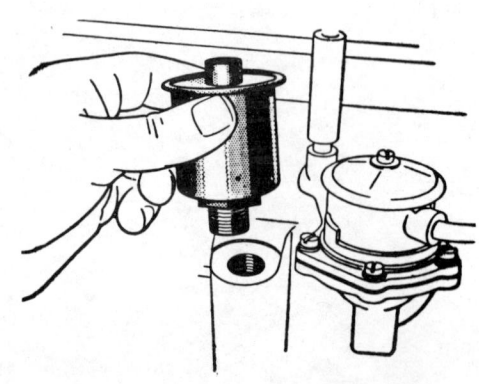

Crankcase ventilation air cleaner

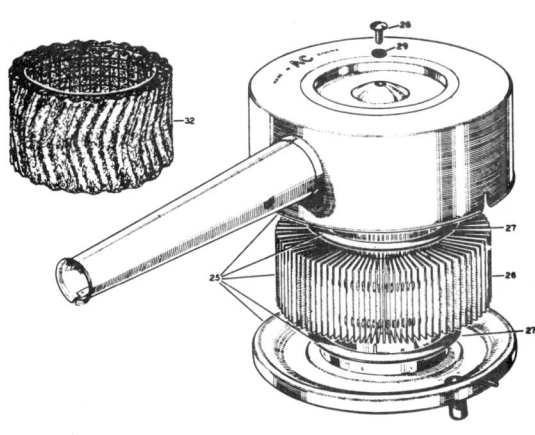

Air cleaner components

25 Body and gasket assembly
26 Paper element
27 Gaskets

28 Screw and washer
29 Screw and washer
32 Washable filter element

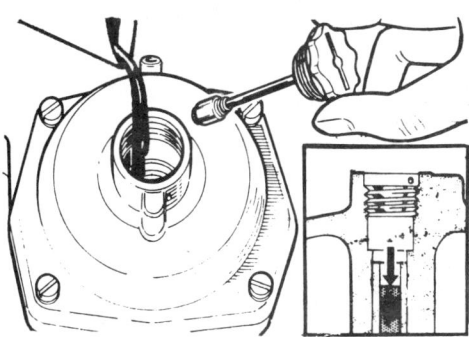

Stromberg carburettor damper level top-up

gasket and cannot get one in time, make one temporarily from cardboard and be careful not to damage it when tightening the plug.

Remove the oil filler cap and pour in 5 pints/ 2.84 litres of Castrol GTX engine oil.

Start the engine but do not rev it until the oil pressure warning light goes out. Leave it ticking over and check that the oil filter housing is not leaking oil. Stop the engine, wait five minutes and check the oil level.

2 Crankcase ventilation air cleaner

Where the engine oil level dipstick enters the engine block there is a cylindrical cartridge which filters air entering the crankcase. Remove the dipstick and unscrew the cartridge, taking care not to lose the rubber sealing ring underneath. Flush it thoroughly in paraffin and shake it dry. Then oil the mesh element with light oil (engine oil). Screw it back into the block - not forgetting the sealing ring- and replace the dipstick.

3 Carburettor air cleaner - paper element type

High performance (90) engines are fitted with carburettor air cleaners made of convoluted paper of a special type. They may also be found fitted on standard models.

On the 90 models remove the whole unit from the carburettor by slackening the clip which holds it to the elbow. Then prise off the cover by twisting a coin in the groove between cover and body.

Lift out the element. It may be cleaned by tapping it on the ends lightly on a flat surface. Any excess accumulations of dust will fall out. Do **not** brush it, dampen it, wash it with petrol or blow it with air jets. Any of these actions will tend to clog up the element.

Clean the inside of the container and cover, replace the element and refix to the carburettor.

4 Carburettor damper (SL90 and 90 models)

The high performance engine is fitted with a Stromberg 150 CD variable choke carburettor. It has a movable piston which is hydraulically damped by oil. To check the oil level, first remove the air cleaner complete with the elbow which joins it to the carburettor. This is done by undoing the two bolts. Do not damage or lose the gasket between the two.

Next remove the plastic cup from the top of the carburettor by unscrewing it and withdrawing it together with the damper rod.

Put a finger in the air intake and lift up the

Solex B30 PSE1-4 carburettor

1 Strangler flap
2 Flap spindle
3 Return spring
4 Flap screw
5 Needle valve and washer
6 Float arm
7 Arm spindle
8 Float
9 Emulsion tube and correction jet
10 Pump injector
11 Sealing ring
12 Pump release valve
13 Main jet
14 Washer
15 Sealing plug
16 Cam return spring
17 Strangler cam assembly
18 Swivel screws
19 Cam pivot
20 Rod—strangler to throttle, and split pins
21 Distance washer
22 Throttle spindle and pump rod lever assembly
23 Pump diaphragm and spring
24 Throttle floating lever
25 Pump cover screw
26 Pump cover
27 Split pin
28 Pump rod spring
29 Strangler bracket bolt
30 Pump rod
31 Cable clip
32 Rod circlips
33 Strangler bracket
34 Idling mixture volume control screw and spring
35 Gaskets
36 Heat insulator
37 Throttle flap and screw
38 Throttle abutment plate
39 Throttle lever
40 Nut
41 Throttle stop screw and spring
42 Pilot jet
43 Body
44 Gasket
45 Float chamber cover
46 Cover screw

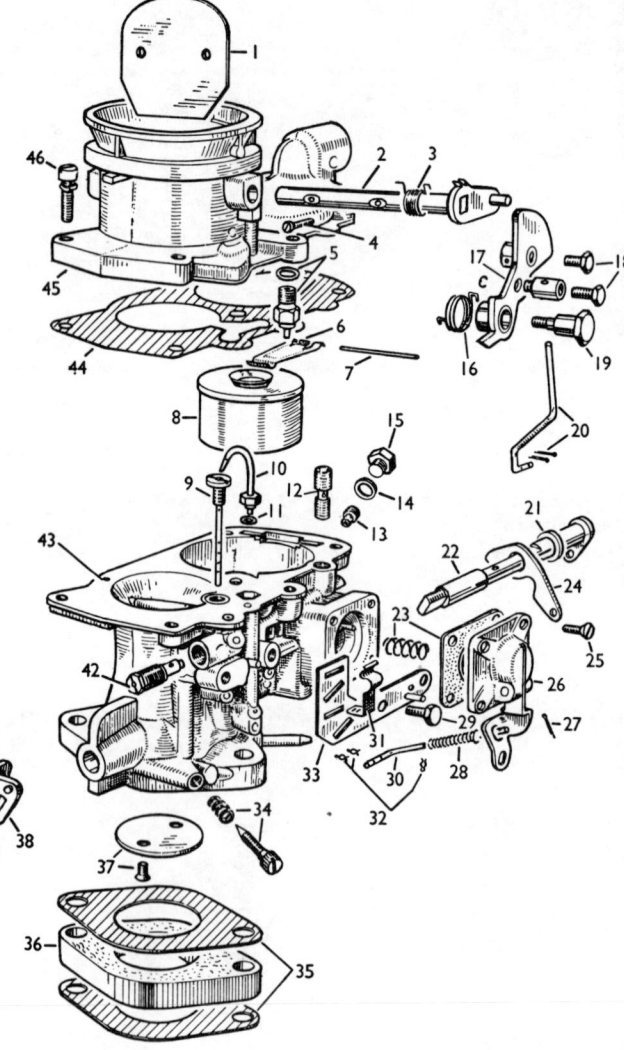

Stromberg 150 CD carburettor

1 Hydraulic damper
2 Washer
3 Bush
4 Retaining ring
5 Cover screws
6 Suction chamber cover
7 Retaining ring screws
8 Diaphragm retaining ring
9 Diaphragm
10 Air valve and guide
11 Metering needle locking screw
12 Metering needle
13 Choke cable clamp screw
14 Throttle flap
15 Throttle flap screws
16 Throttle return spring
17 Throttle stop screw spring
18 Throttle stop screw
19 Fast idle control screw
20 Locknut
21 Throttle
22 Lockwasher
23 Throttle spindle nut
24 Starter bar spring
25 Choke cam lever
26 Choke lever
27 Lockwasher
28 Choke lever nut
29 Choke lever spring
30 Float fulcrum pin
31 Needle seating washer
32 Needle seating
33 Float chamber screw-long
34 Float chamber screws-short
35 Float chamber
36 Jet adjuster
37 Sealing ring
38 Float arm
39 Float
40 Jet bush retainer
41 Sealing ring
42 Gasket
43 Starter bar retainer
44 Starter bar
45 Throttle stop
46 Throttle spindle
47 Main body
48 Air valve lifting pin clip
49 Spring
50 Air valve lifting pin
51 Jet
52 Spring
53 Washer
54 Sealing ring
55 Bush
56 Washer
57 Air valve return spring

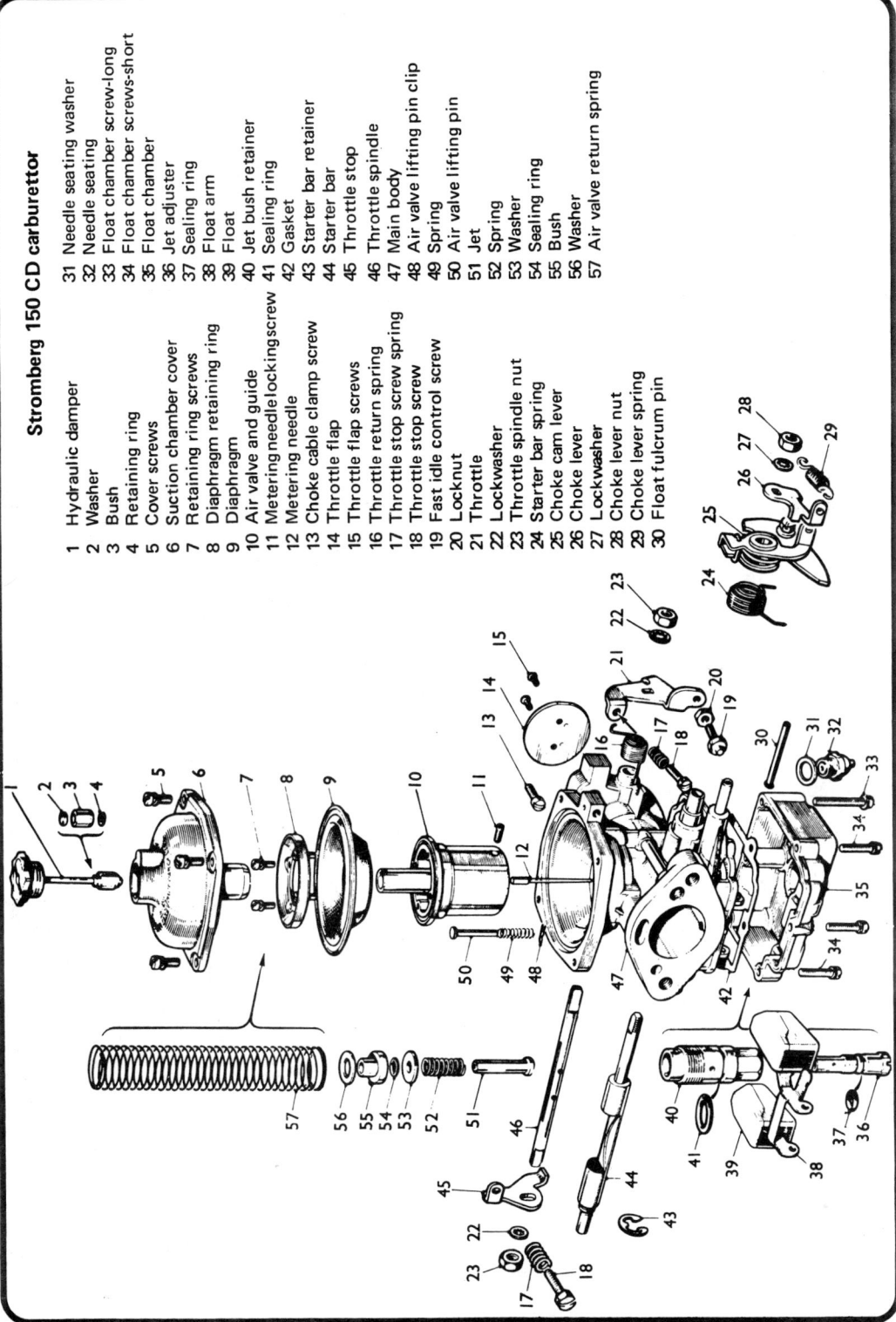

piston so you can see into the top of the hollow guide rod from above. The rod should be full of engine oil to within ¼ inch/6 mm of the top of the rod.

Replace the damper rod into the carburettor. On some models there is a small collar on the damper rod which has to locate into the top of the hollow guide tube of the piston. To do this, lift up the piston with a finger, insert the damper and collar and then lower the piston and damper together, and screw down the damper cap. Then lift the piston fully again to push the collar right home into the top of the guide tube. You can check that this has been done properly by lifting the piston and unscrewing and lifting the cap just far enough to see the top of the guide tube.

Refit the air cleaner.

5 Fuel pump

The fuel pump is fitted with a wire gauze screen to prevent particles of foreign matter reaching the carburettor. It does not prevent very fine particles.

As the pump (below the coil on the left hand side of the engine) is lower than the fuel tank, the first thing to do is remove the flexible horizontal input pipe by pulling it off. Then plug it with a pencil or clamp it with a self-grip wrench to prevent petrol draining out.

Remove the screw in the centre of the top cover and lift off the cover, tubular nylon distance piece, sealing ring and gauze filter. Clean the gauze with petrol and by blowing through it to clear all the holes in the mesh. Do **not** wipe it with anything from which strands could get caught in the mesh. If possible clean the body of the carburettor with a small brush. There will possibly be small accumulations of grit to be seen.

Replace the filter screen followed by the sealing ring nylon distance piece and top cover. Make sure the sealing ring is in good condition. When the screw is replaced do not overtighten it. If you strip the thread, your car will be immobilised until either a new thread is tapped, a larger screw is found or a new pump fitted.

Run the engine and look to see that there are no leaks.

6 Spark plugs - remove, clean and reset

Pull off one spark plug lead and with the proper tubular spanner remove the plug. Do not remove all the leads at once or you may get them mixed up. Do not use a makeshift spanner

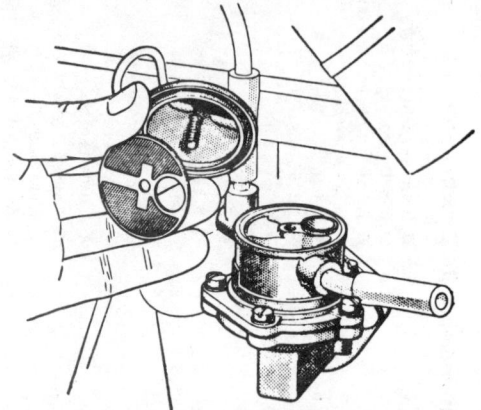
Fuel pump filter

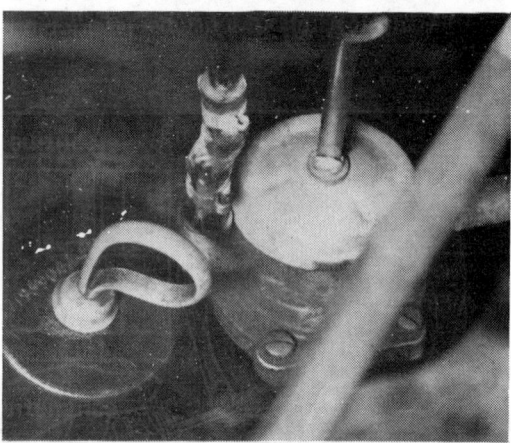
Fuel pump location

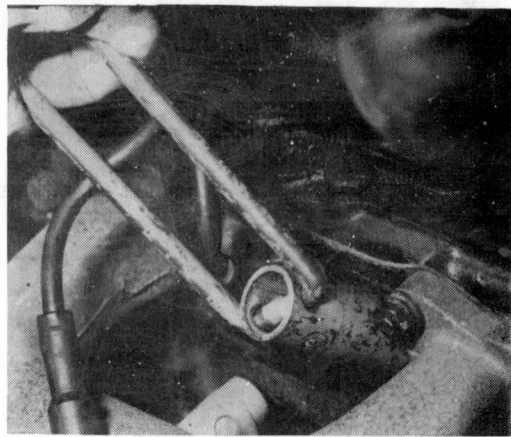
Spark plug removal

Sample spark plugs

Plug too hot - white deposits

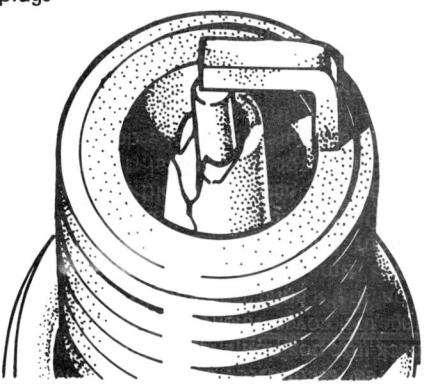

A chipped electrode

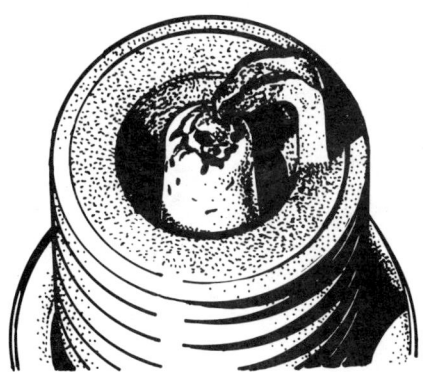

Typical damage caused by pre-ignition

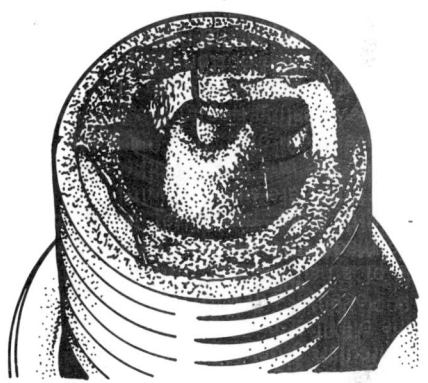

Plug too cold - dry black deposits

Badly burnt electrode

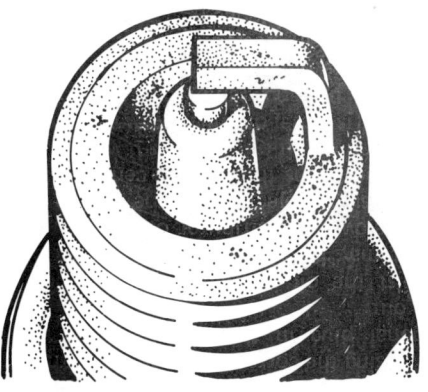

A normal plug with light tan deposits

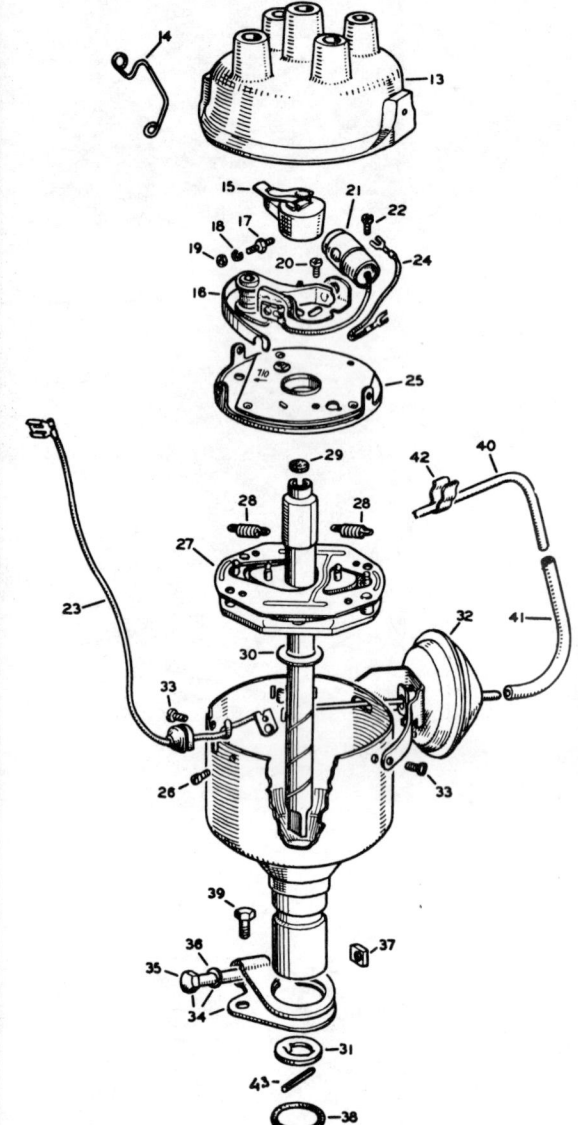

Distributor components

13 Distributor cap
14 Distributor cap retaining clip
15 Rotor arm
16 Contact set
17 Contact arm stud, washer)
18 and nut   )
19   )
20 Fixed contact locking screw
21 Condenser
22 Condenser fixing screw
23 LT lead (with grommet) coil to contact
24 Lead - earth
25 Contact breaker plate assembly
26 Contact plate fixing screw
27 Mainshaft & cam assembly
28 Balance weight springs
29 Felt pad
30 Upper washer, mainshaft
31 Lower retaining washer mainshaft
32 Vacuum advance unit
33 Vacuum unit fixing screw
34 Distributor clamping ring assem.
35 Clamping bolt, washer and nut
36 Clamping bolt, washer and nut
37 Clamping bolt, washer and nut
38 Oil seal ring
39 Distributor clamp fixing screw
40 Suction pipe elbow (rigid)
41 Suction pipe flexible
42 Clip
43 Mainshaft locating pin

Distributor cap segment inspection

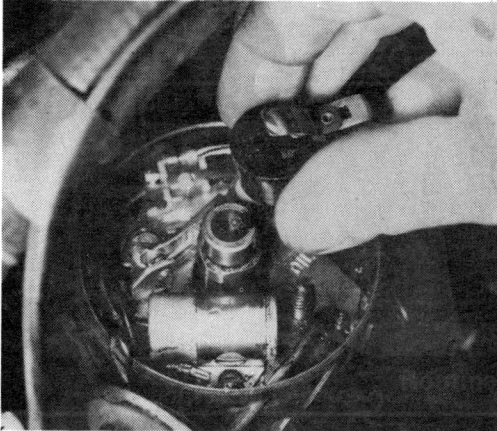

Rotor arm removal

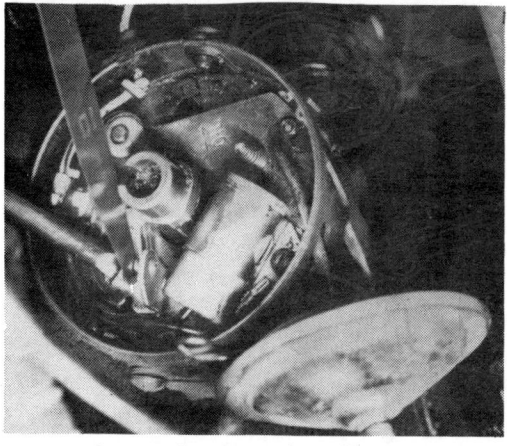

Contact breaker point adjustment

or you will probably break the plug.

The plugs should be dry at the electrode points. If they are oily there is something wrong with your engine (worn piston rings or bores) and it will almost certainly be using a lot of oil.

Clean the electrode with a wire brush to remove any deposits. If you can get to a garage which has a special machine for sand blasting them and testing the spark under pressure, so much the better.

The gap between the central electrode and the horizontal one should be .030 inch/.75 mm. The gap can be reduced by tapping the horizontal electrode nearer to the centre one. If the gap has to be increased avoid putting any strain on the central electrode or you may crack the ceramic insulation which surrounds it.

Before replacing the plugs, clean the seats in the engine where they will fit, taking great care not to inadvertently push any particles inside the hole.

Make sure that each plug has a sealing washer and replace the plug firmly but not overtight.

7 Distributor contact breaker points

More starting and poor running problems are caused by dirty or maladjusted points than anything else.

Remove the distributor cap by pushing back the two wire clips, one at each side, and lifting it off. Tuck the cap out of the way to one side.

Remove the rotor arm by lifting it straight up. Do not pull it by the spring contact on top. It can be quite tight so you may have to pull hard.

The two contacts may now be seen clearly, one of which is on a leaf spring which is moved by the 4 point cam on the central spindle. If the car is now put in top gear and the handbrake released, it can be moved so that the spindle turns and the cam will move the spring contact away from the fixed one. When the gap is at its greatest it can be measured with a feeler gauge blade. The gap should be .020 inch/0.5 mm and must not vary more than .002 either way otherwise the ignition timing will be affected. In order to see the faces of the two contacts more easily the spring contact can be pushed away from the other with a small screwdriver. If they should be oily, then clean the whole area with petrol. If one face should have a small hard lump on it with a corresponding recess in the opposite face it will be impossible to set the points accurately with a feeler blade. Ideally the points should be renewed or at least taken out for cleaning up. It is possible to eliminate the small peak by carefully working on it with fine emery but this will be a fiddle, and care needs to be taken to keep the dust from getting into the distributor body. To adjust the gap slacken the screw which holds the fixed contact point bracket. The fixed contact can then be moved one way or the other (there is a pair of notches to assist in this). The gap is correct when the feeler blade is felt to touch both contact surfaces lightly. If the blade touches too firmly, it means that the contacts are sprung apart by the feeler blade and that, when the blade is removed, the gap will close to something smaller than it should be.

Tighten the locking screw firmly and then check the gap again. Replace the rotor arm, noting that the lug in the rotor recess engages fully in the cut-out in the spindle. Once again, be careful not to bend or distort the contact blade on the rotor arm. The inside of the distributor cap should be examined before replacement. See that the five contact terminals are clean and wipe the cap out with a dry cloth. When fitting the distributor cover see that it fits flush before replacing the fixing clips.

8 Fan belt

The fan belt drives three things - the fan, the water pump and the generator. In order that all three may continue to work properly the belt must be neither too slack nor too tight. (Over-tightness imposes strain on the pump and generator bearings).

The generator can be moved in order to alter the tension. First check the tension by pressing the belt with the thumb between fan and generator pulleys. It should depress ¼ inch/ 6 mm. To alter the tension, slacken the two pivot mounting bolts and both bolts underneath the generator, securing the slotted brace. The generator can then be swung out to tighten the belt using a lever to assist if necessary.

Provided the mounting bolts have not been slackened too far, the generator will be easy to hold in position whilst the bolts are tightened again.

9 Valve clearances

The manufacturers say that the valve clearances should be checked and set whilst the engine is running. Unless you have had a lot of practice this can be difficult and liable to cause damage so the procedure given here is with the engine static. The engine should be thoroughly

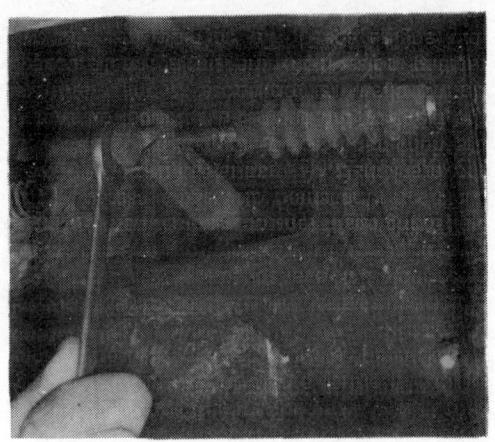

Clutch adjustment locknut

Valve rocker arm clearance adjustment

A socket must be used to loosen/tighten self-locking nuts

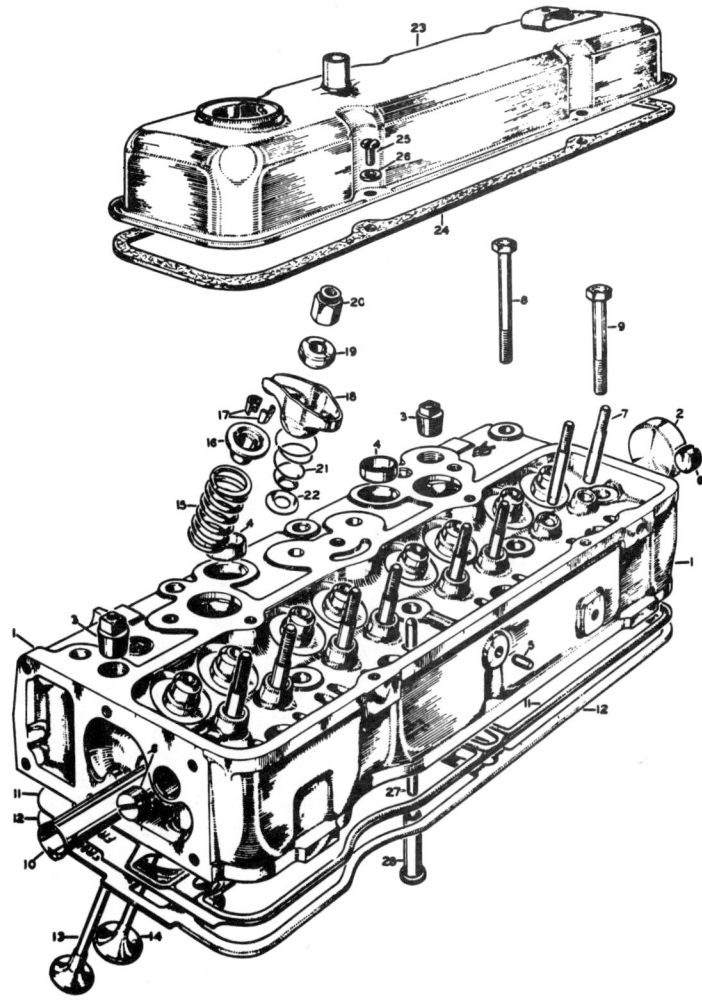

Cylinder head components

1	Cylinder head	11	Cylinder head gasket-high)	21 Retaining spring
2	Plug (cooling gallery)	12	or low compression)	22 Shim
3	Plug (if heater pipe not fitted)	13	Exhaust valve	23 Rocker cover
4	Plug (cooling gallery)	14	Inlet valve	24 Cover gasket
5	Plug (oil hole)	15	Valve spring	25 Screw and washer - rocker)
6	Plug (oil gallery)	16	Spring cap	26 cover)
7	Stud - rocker arm	17	Collets (split collar)	27 Push rod
8	Bolt - cylinder head	18	Rocker arm	28 Tappet
9	Bolt - cylinder head	19	Rocker ball	
10	Tube - water	20	Rocker nut	

warmed up to normal operating temperature (5 to 10 minutes from cold). It is a good idea to have a new rocker cover gasket available.

Remove the air cleaner for easier access and remove the wires and hose which are clipped to the rocker cover. Then undo the four securing screws and carefully lift off the cover and gasket. If the gasket is broken, or is hard and brittle, it is best to use a new one on replacement.

Valve clearances are checked between the end of the valve stem and the rocker arm and this gap occurs when the valve is fully closed. The engine will need turning over and this is done with a spanner fitted on the nut in the centre of the crankshaft pulley - the one at the bottom driving the fan belt. There are eight valves and for this procedure they are numbered from 1 to 8 starting at the front of the engine. Not all have the same clearance.

Each valve is fully closed when a corresponding one is fully open (ie when the rocker presses it fully down against the spring) and the table following shows this relationship. If the order is followed as shown the sequence will avoid unnecessary turning of the engine which can be tedious. The correct clearance for each valve is shown. A feeler blade of the correct thickness should be inserted in each gap in turn accordingly. The gap is correct when a slight drag is felt on the blade when it is pulled through. To adjust the gap involves rotating the nut in the centre of the rocker arm and for this a tubular spanner must be used which does not foul the rocker arm when it is fitted over the nut. If the gap is too small to insert the feeler blade turn the nut anticlockwise until the blade goes in and the gap is set. To close the gap turn the nut clockwise.

Valve being checked	Clearance	Corresponding valve open
No 1	.010 inch	No 8
3	.006 inch	6
5	.010 inch	4
2	.006 inch	7
8	.010 inch	1
6	.006 inch	3
4	.010 inch	5
7	.006 inch	2

Note: On 90 engines all valve clearances are .008 inch.

10 Handbrake, throttle and clutch linkages

If the accelerator pedal is moved, the linkages to the carburettor inside the engine compartment can readily be located. A few drops of Castrol Everyman or engine oil should be applied to the joints. Similarly, if one gets underneath the car and asks someone to operate the clutch and handbrake, the various moving parts may be lubricated.

11 Gearbox oil level

On the left hand side of the gearbox a square headed plug can be found which is the combined level and filler plug. Unless you have a pit or ramp it is difficult to check the level exactly because to get at the plug the car has to be jacked up and the oil will then not be level. However, place the car on level ground, jack it up on the left hand side, get underneath and thoroughly clean the area round the filler plug before removing it. There is little point in fiddling about trying to see where the level is so add Castrol ST Gear Oil from one of their dispensers with a convenient flexible filler pipe. Continue until the oil overflows and then let the car down off the jack. As you jacked up on the left side the gearbox will be slightly overfull so wait now until all overflow stops. Then jack the car up again and replace the filler/level plug firmly. Do not overfill the gearbox as too much oil will cause pressure build-up, forcing oil out onto the clutch housing or through the rear oil seal which does no good at all. Do not put the wrong kind of oil in the gearbox either. There is no drain plug.

12 Rear axle oil level

The rear axle oil level and filler plug is set in the centre of the axle on the differential housing cover. It is accessible without having to jack the car up. Stand the car on level ground and clean around the plug thoroughly before removing it. Using Castrol Hypoy 90 from their convenient flexible dispenser, add oil until it overflows from the hole. Leave it a few minutes until the overflow stops and then replace the plug. Do not overfill with oil as it will only come out through the vent plug on the top of the axle casing (right hand side). It is worthwhile checking that this vent plug is clear. If blocked, pressure can build up and blow out the oil seals.

13 Carburettor - slow running adjustment

If the engine idles unevenly or keeps stopping

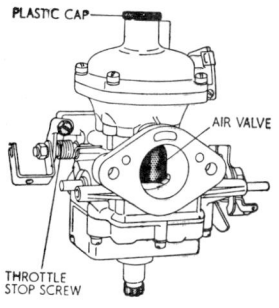

Stromberg 150 CD throttle stop screw

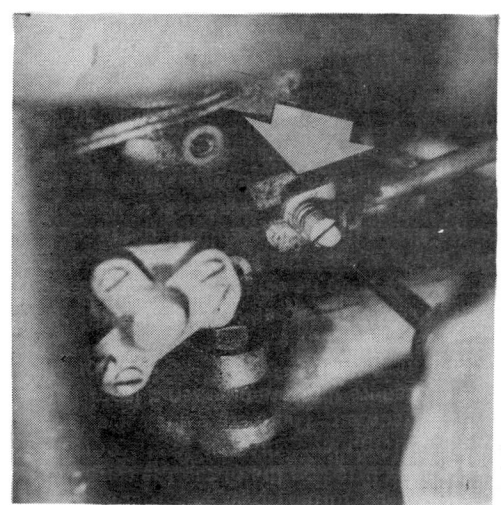

Throttle stop screw (arrowed)

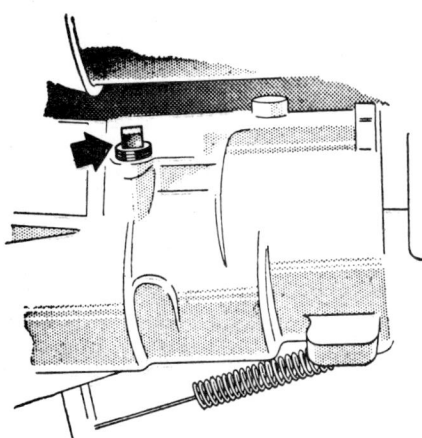

Gearbox combined oil level and filler plug

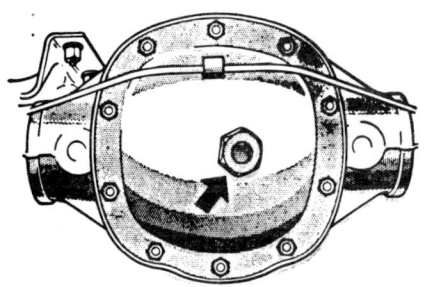

Rear axle combined oil level and filler plug

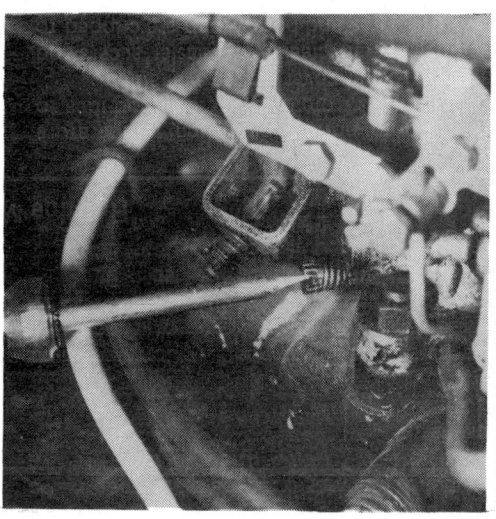

Mixture adjustment screw

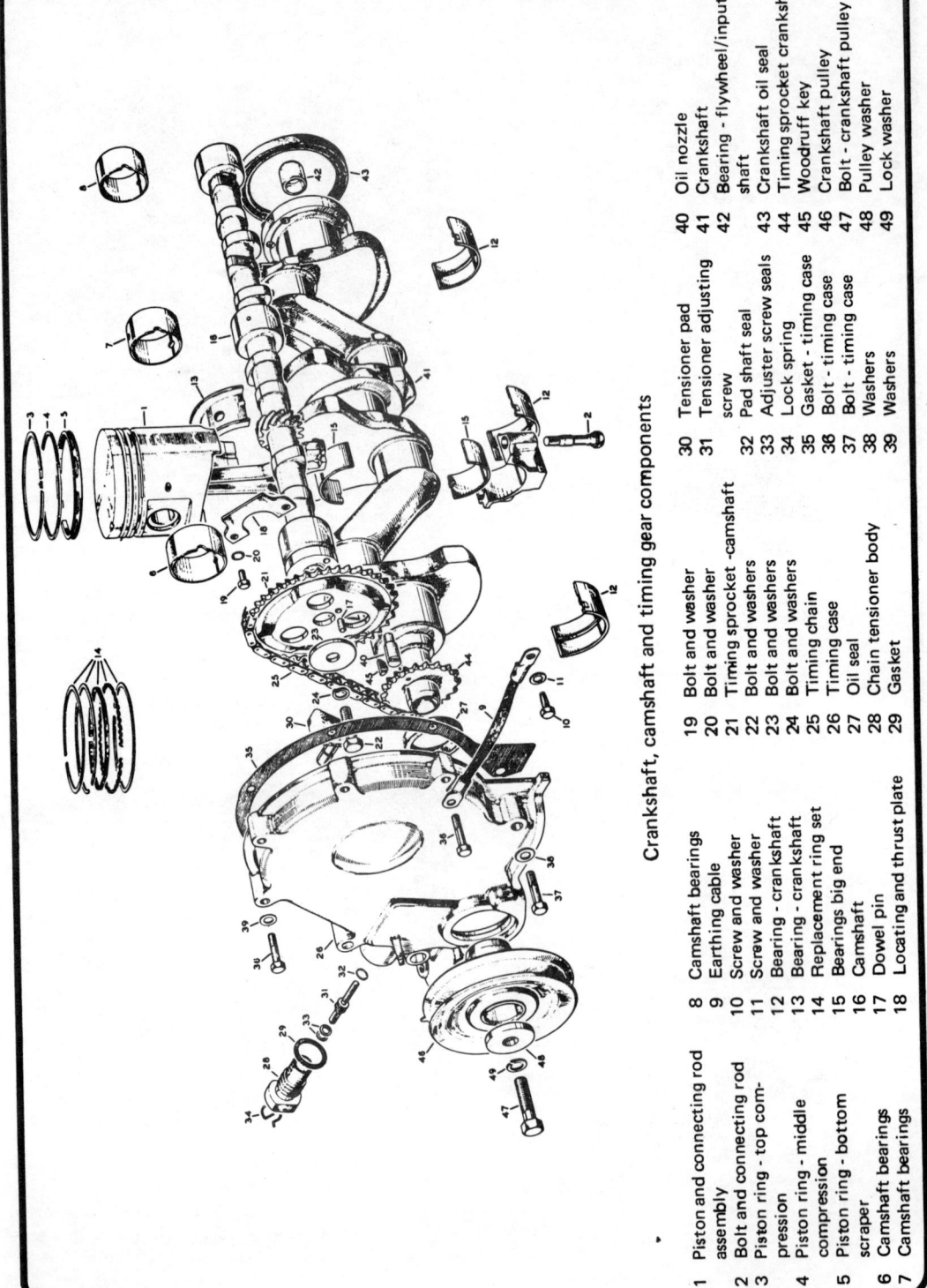

Crankshaft, camshaft and timing gear components

1 Piston and connecting rod assembly
2 Bolt and connecting rod
3 Piston ring - top compression
4 Piston ring - middle compression
5 Piston ring - bottom scraper
6 Camshaft bearings
7 Camshaft bearings
8 Camshaft bearings
9 Earthing cable
10 Screw and washer
11 Screw and washer
12 Bearing - crankshaft
13 Bearing - crankshaft
14 Replacement ring set
15 Bearings big end
16 Camshaft
17 Dowel pin
18 Locating and thrust plate
19 Bolt and washer
20 Bolt and washer
21 Timing sprocket -camshaft
22 Bolt and washers
23 Bolt and washers
24 Bolt and washers
25 Timing chain
26 Timing case
27 Oil seal
28 Chain tensioner body
29 Gasket
30 Tensioner pad
31 Tensioner adjusting screw
32 Pad shaft seal
33 Adjuster screw seals
34 Lock spring
35 Gasket - timing case
36 Bolt - timing case
37 Bolt - timing case
38 Washers
39 Washers
40 Oil nozzle
41 Crankshaft
42 Bearing - flywheel/input shaft
43 Crankshaft oil seal
44 Timing sprocket crankshaft
45 Woodruff key
46 Crankshaft pulley
47 Bolt - crankshaft pulley
48 Pulley washer
49 Lock washer

on tick-over it may be due to a small maladjustment on the carburettor. First get the engine completely warmed up. Then screw in the throttle stop screw on the carburettor so that the engine runs quickly enough to avoid stalling. Then turn the mixture control screw anticlockwise until the speed of the engine 'hunts' - that is speeds up in intermittent but regular bursts. Then turn the same screw clockwise until the engine runs evenly. It will now be running too fast so the throttle stop screw should be turned anticlockwise to reduce the engine speed. If when the engine speed drops the 'hunting' resumes, screw the mixture control in a little further.

Do not try and get the tick-over too slow - better a little too fast if anything. The Viva engine is high revving by design and is fussy at low tick-over speeds.

On 90 engines the principle of adjustment is the same but the jet adjuster (in place of the mixture control screw) is mounted in the base of the carburettor and if it is altered it means that the performance of the carburettor is altered at all engine speeds - not just tick-over. The basic setting of the jet adjusting screw is three turns open. To check this it is necessary first to remove the air cleaner complete with elbow. Then put a finger in the air intake to hold down the piston and screw in the jet adjusting screw until it touches the bottom of the piston. Then undo it three complete turns. Replace the air cleaner, run the engine until warm and then set the throttle stop screw to a fast idle speed. Adjust the jet mixture screw until the engine runs evenly. Any adjustment should not exceed ½ turn in either direction. If uneven running is still apparent it must be being caused by something else.

Re-adjust the throttle stop screw to give a reasonable tick-over speed.

14 Timing chain tensioner adjustment

The timing chain drives the camshaft from the crankshaft. A manual adjuster is fitted in the right hand side of the timing chain cover at the front of the engine. An indication that the timing chain is too loose is an intermittent rattling noise from the timing chain cover at low engine speed. To correct this, the small square headed manual adjustment screw should be turned anticlockwise in progressions of a ¼ turn until the rattling stops. Overtightening will be indicated by a whining noise replacing the rattle.

15 Clutch pedal free play adjustment

Wear in the clutch will not be indicated by any significant change in the operation of the pedal but, if the cable is not checked and adjusted, the thrust release bearing could be subjected to unnecessary wear.

To adjust the cable, jack up the car and locate the end of the cable where it fits into the clutch operating lever. Unhook the return spring from the lever and move the lever in the opposite direction of the return spring action and at the same time pull the end of the cable in the other direction. There should be a ¼ inch gap between the two. To increase the gap, undo the locknut and rotate the ball ended adjuster as required. Tighten the locknut and reconnect the return spring after the adjustment has been made.

16 Check brake lining material and adjust brakes

Examination of disc brake pads is described in the 'S' Service, Item 5, Page 28.

To examine the linings of drum brake shoes, removal of the drums is necessary. Jack up the car and remove the road wheel. The drum is held to the hub by two hexagonal headed bolts which should be removed. Slacken off the brake adjusters two or three 'clicks' (see Service 'S'). The drum can now, in theory, be pulled straight off. More than likely it will stick, either on the hub or at the roots of the wheel studs. Use a little penetrating oil to ease these spots and, if you have to tap the drum a little, use only a soft headed mallet or a block of wood.

With the drum removed, brush off all the dust from the linings and from inside the drum. The linings and contact surface of the drum should be smooth and no traces of oil should be visible. Each lining is held in place by eight rivets and the heads of these rivets should be recessed at least .025 inch. If less, the linings should be renewed as soon as possible. If the linings have worn too far, the rivets will have scored the surface of the drum. In such instances new linings and a new drum and hub may be needed also.

17 Brake servo air filter - renewal

On top of the servo unit there is a plastic cylindrical housing held in position with a wire hoop clip. When the cover is lifted, the element can be removed. Always fit a new element. The old one cannot be cleaned. Wipe out the interior of the cover and the base before fitting the new element.

18 Generator rear bush - lubrication

At the rear of the generator there is a cavity in the centre of the shaft bearing housing. A few drops of Castrol Everyman or GTX should be put into the hole to lubricate the special porous bush.

Front suspension grease points

SERVICE 'B'

Complete Service 'A' except when the items given below modify certain procedures.

1 Carburettor air cleaners (wire gauze type)

The wire gauze type cleaner is fitted to all standard engines. If a paper element is fitted instead, carburettor jets and settings will need recalibration. Slacken the clip securing the unit to the carburettor and detach the rubber breather hose. Remove the cover by either undoing the screw or unclipping it with a coin round the edge.

Remove the wire gauze element and flush it thoroughly in paraffin or petrol. Let it dry and then dip it in clean engine oil. Let the surplus oil drain off. Thoroughly clean out the interior of the filter housing and intake pipe before replacing the filter element.

When the unit is refitted, the intake pipe (if it is of the movable type) may be positioned on the exhaust manifold in winter months.

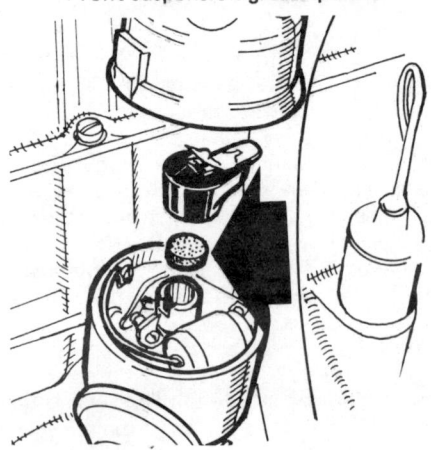

Distributor lubrication

2 Carburettor air cleaners (paper element type)

Proceed as described in Service 'A', Item 3, Page 35, except that the paper elements should be discarded and new ones fitted.

3 Front suspension ball joints

Each of the steering joints, two at each side, has a grease nipple in order that lubrication may be carried out. Access to them is easier if the wheel is removed unless a pit or ramp is available. The joints should first be cleaned off and the rubber gaiters examined to make sure they are intact.

A few shots of grease with a molybdenum disulphide additive (Castrol MS3) from a grease gun are all that is needed. Do not over lubricate in order to see grease ooze out. It will only ooze out when the rubber gaiters have either burst or are not fitting correctly. If the gaiters are in poor condition, have them attended to at a garage together with the joints themselves.

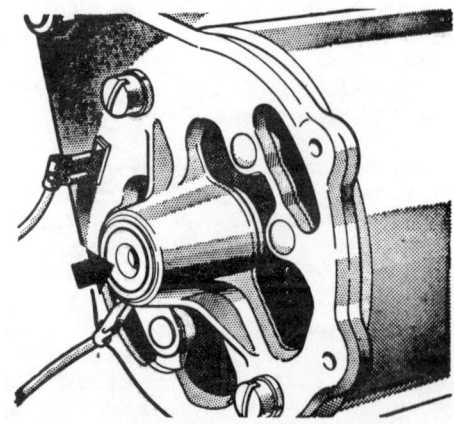

Dynamo rear bush - lubrication

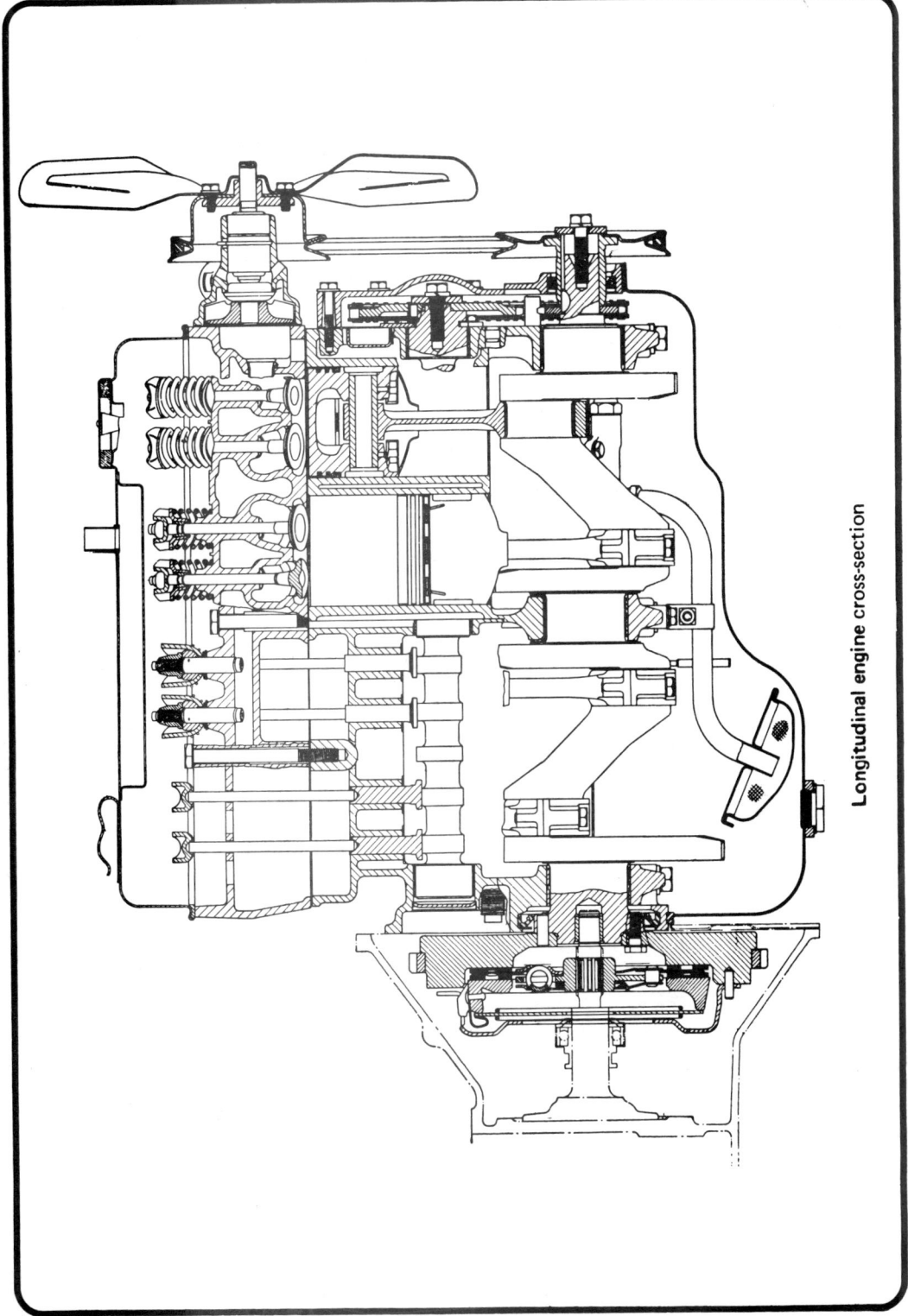

Longitudinal engine cross-section

4 Distributor - lubrication

Remove the distributor cap and rotor arm as described in Service 'A', Item 7, Page 41. In the top of the spindle, a felt pad will be seen. This should be impregnated with one or two drops of light oil (Castrol Everyman or GTX). At the same time 10 to 12 drops should be added through the hole in the baseplate.

SERVICE 'C'

In view of the size and importance of this service which occurs only once every 24 months it is recommended that a complete professional check be carried out by an authorised Vauxhall dealer.

Their experience will enable them to pinpoint certain defects or modifications which may not be covered in the normal scope of routine maintenance. Such a service would normally be combined with a Service 'S' if you were not in the habit of sending your car for garage servicing regularly.

The two main items not covered by the 'B' Service which occur on this check, are the hydraulic system overhaul and the removal and repacking with grease of the front wheel bearings. Both these call for more detailed dismantling and checking which is not within the scope of this manual. The companion Owner's Workshop Manual gives full details.

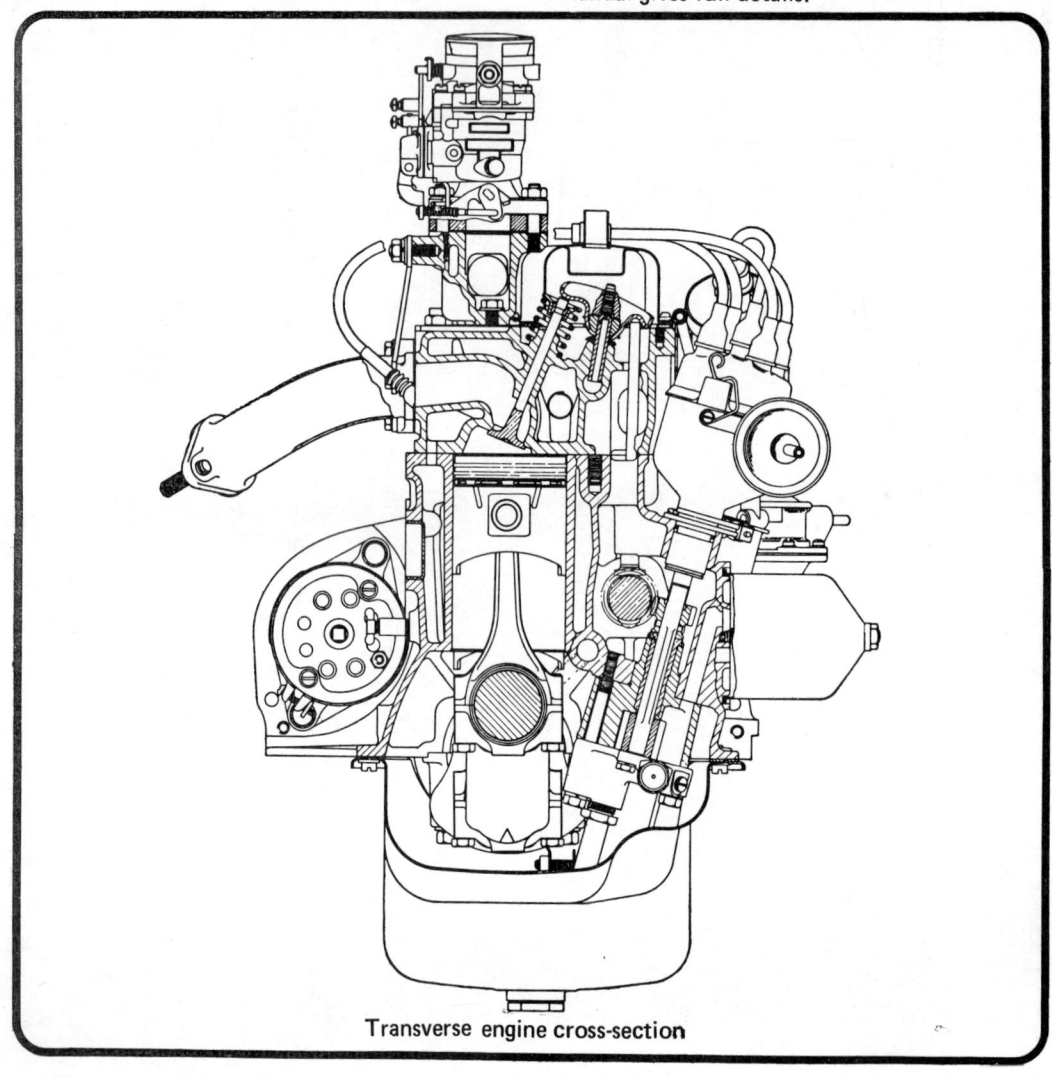

Transverse engine cross-section

Bodywork maintenance, cleaning and minor repairs

Introduction

Most owners like their cars to look clean and well polished with a freedom from rust. Not only does regular cleaning show up stone chips and rust marks which can be easily attended to before getting worse, but also ensures the appearance is maintained which results in a good resale value for the car.

Regular car cleaning is regarded by many as a necessary evil. Others enjoy this aspect of car care far more than the routine mechanical maintenance. The secret really is to keep the car clean all the time so that it is not allowed to become too dirty, making the work all that more difficult.

If you do not feel like doing the job all at one go then divide it into sections as we have done here in this Chapter. Do a little each week. This will give a continuous cleaning programme and enable you to do other jobs as well so as to break the monotony.

Should the car have been recently acquired and be in a dirty state then take it along to a suitably equipped garage and have the whole of the underside and engine compartment steam cleaned. This will save a tremendous amount of time - it is a very dirty job without proper equipment. It will not take long and is well worth it.

Car cleaning - interior

Many owners leave interior cleaning to last and wash the exterior first. This is working backwards because the dust created by removal of carpets will only settle on the clean exterior.

By regularly cleaning the interior the upholstery will remain looking nearly new, the mats or carpets fresh and clean and the general appearance smart and well cared for. When the carpeting is removed any water leaks will be evident and corrective action can be taken before rust sets in.

First empty the car completely - from shelves and trays to under the seats - of all the paraphernalia of travel.

Lift out the rubber mats, carpeting and underfelt. The rubber mats should be washed. The carpets may be brushed, shaken or beaten to remove the dust and dirt. If badly marked they can be cleaned using a carpet shampoo. Remember that they must be dried thoroughly so choose your time for doing this. They may need drying overnight. Underfelt should be carefully shaken but not washed and beaten otherwise it will be difficult to dry and start to break up. If the carpeting around the pedals is worn it is recommended that it be renewed as it can be a danger especially for lady drivers wearing heeled shoes.

With a stiff handbrush or a vacuum cleaner with a flexible hose, remove all traces of dust and grit that is left inside.

For cleaning the upholstery materials and panels on the doors, use a detergent liquid in a water solution. Do not overwet the areas being cleaned as you do not want interior padding to get soaked. It will smell or rot if it does. Stubborn marks or ingrained dirt should be shifted with a soft bristled brush. An old nailbrush is ideal.

When finished, wipe the surfaces as dry as possible and leave the windows open to air the car out. It is not advisable to do any interior car cleaning using water in wet weather - it takes too long to dry out.

When cleaning windows and screens, use plain water and a chamois leather. A little household ammonia in the water prevents smears.

Never put damp carpets back in the car. If you are in a hurry to use the car leave them out until dry. Otherwise they will not dry properly and will get dirty again more quickly. They will deteriorate more quickly too.

Check that the door drain holes on the bottom edge are clear. These holes are not just to let water out of the door that may get inside by mistake. It is impossible to keep water out in wet weather so the holes are not just an emergency measure.

Next check nuts, bolts and screws and

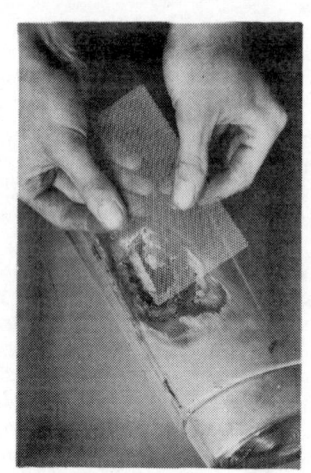
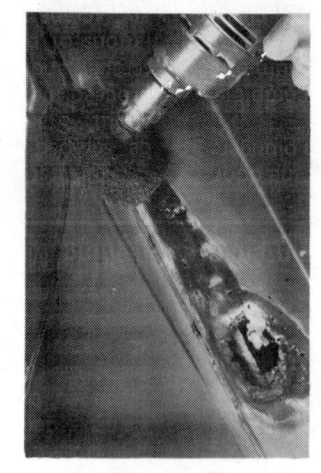
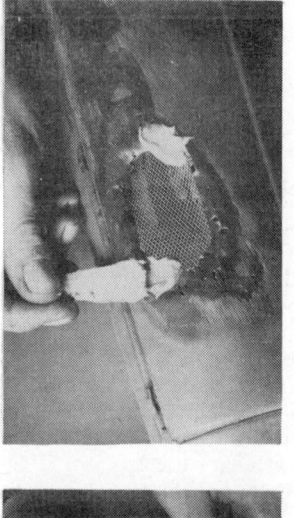
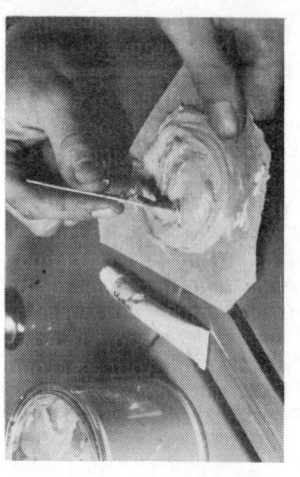

The first half of a body repair sequence - cutting away and fibreglass filling

make sure that all are tight. Lubricate the door locks and hinges, courtesy light switch plunger, choke control and front seat runners.

Turning to the boot, remove the complete contents including spare wheel, and vacuum out all the dust and dirt. Wipe the paintwork down with a damp cloth. If carpeting is fitted, clean this as well in a similar manner to the interior carpeting. Again look for water leaks especially in the corners.

Using an oil can, lubricate the handbrake lever assembly and the pedal pivots. Inspect the pedal rubbers for signs of excessive wear and fit new ones if necessary. It is dangerous to drive with worn pedal rubbers - on a wet day it is easy for the foot to accidentally slip off.

Should you have a slight tear on one of the seats or trim panel, cut a piece of spare trim from the underside of one of the seats and apply a coat of impact adhesive such as clear Bostik. Insert the patch into the hole with the glue uppermost and then apply adhesive to the flap of the torn section. Allow the recommended drying time to pass and then press down the torn edges trying to get the edges as close together as possible which will make the repair less pronounced. Any large tears will have to be repaired using a piece of matching material.

The time has now come for touching up the interior paintwork and full details for this will be found later on in this Chapter. Once the paint is dry the rear seat cushion and carpeting may be refitted followed by the oddments that live on the parcel shelf and in the boot.

This is a good time to check the contents of the first aid kit, if carried, and any deficiencies should be made up. Check the tools. Lubricate the threads of the jack. Stow away the contents of the boot, making sure that the main tool kit is so situated where it will not slide around or rattle.

Car cleaning - exterior (underside)

It was recommended in the introduction to this Chapter that if the car is in a dirty state it be steam cleaned if possible. If it is not possible then you must prepare for a quite long and very dirty job. You will need paraffin, water (preferably a hose) a wire brush, stiff bristle brush and a scraper.

Remove the carpets from the car and boot and jack up the car as high as possible at one end or at one side and take off the wheels that are raised. If you can jack up the whole car so much the better.

The first job is to scrape off that which can be scraped - this before sloshing any liquids about. Start from one end or one side and proceed methodically and particularly with the scraper and wire brush as appropriate. Coagulations of oily mud will clog the brush so try and scrape this and use the brush only for dry and awkward bits. Sweep up the scrapings and dispose of them before going to the next stage. Having scraped off all that can be scraped, the body floor pan should be washed off with water - scrubbing as necessary with a bristle brush. Do not use paraffin except in areas which are oil covered as this will make preparation of the surface for undersealing difficult. All mechanical parts which are not subject to rust can be flushed clean with paraffin using a brush and rag.

Finally hose off and then examine the car interior to see what leaks there may be. This was the reason for removing the floor coverings. Check that all pipes and other items are secured to the floor pan.

When dry, rusty patches should be brushed free of loose material and treated with a good rust arrester such as 'Kurust'. Then apply a good body underseal compound for future protection. Do not put the compound on any moving parts or unions, nuts and bolts which may need undoing some time.

Car cleaning - exterior

Once a week the exterior of the car should be washed and wiped dry. For this job a flexibrush on the end of the garden hose is ideal, a sponge to assist wiping down and a leather to finish the operation off.

First make sure that all windows and doors are closed. Thoroughly soak the car in water using a gentle spray. Once the dirt has been loosened by the water wipe down the panels using the brush with water still running through it - this way the paintwork should not be scratched by the dirt.

Next apply wax car shampoo or a little washing up liquid, working from the roof downwards. Any dead flies, marks or tar may be removed using a drop of paraffin on a cloth. Do not forget to clean the wing mirrors, front grille, the wiper arms and, of course, the wheels.

Finally rinse off with plenty of clean water and wipe dry using a leather. Brightwork is cleaned in the same way. Occasionally one of the special polishes which can be obtained for

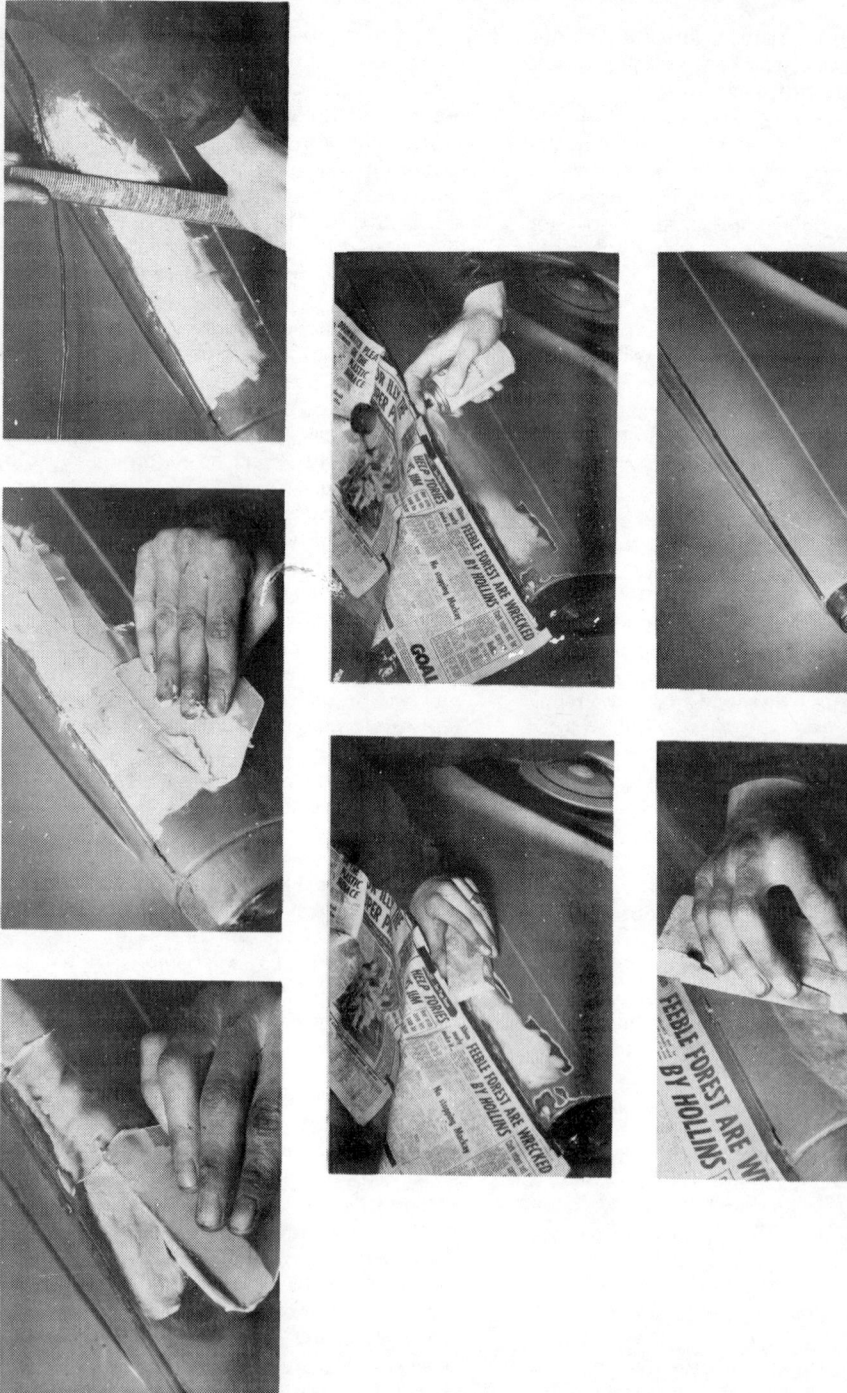

The second body repair sequence - filing and finishing

chromium plating may be used but on no account use an ordinary metal polish.

Every six months it is recommended that the exterior be wax polished. There are, however, several important points to be noted before polish is used on a car.

1 If the paint is new do not polish for at least two months, to allow the paint to dry fully and harden.

2 Do not use a cutting paste to remove the dull film from cars which have been sprayed with a metallic paint.

3 When purchasing a wax polish, always make sure that it is suitable for the type of paintwork on the car.

4 Do not attempt to wax polish a car in the sun or when the body is still warm, having been in the sun. It will look awful and possibly damage the paint surface.

5 After washing the car, make sure the surface is thoroughly dry before applying any polish. If it is a damp day, wait for a dry one.

Finally a few don'ts so as to avoid deterioration of the paintwork.

Don't dust or polish a dirty car. Always wash.

Don't get polish or wax on any of the glass.

Don't park under trees especially in the hot sun or when raining.

Don't use a cutting compound or haze remover on cars finished with an acrylic paint.

Bodywork - paint touch-up

On any modern car with an all steel body the greatest enemy of all is rust and this is most likely to start under the wings or along the sills. The revolving road wheels fling water, mud and grit onto the paint surface and it will only be a matter of time before the paint skin is penetrated and rusting starts.

It is for this reason that many new cars are given a thick coat of underseal, usually of a bituminous or rubber base, to guard against rusting. However, if this was the end of the story paint maintenance would be relatively simple. Unfortunately it is not because chips appear at the front of the wings, along the outside of the wing panels and doors, as well as the edges of the bonnet and boot lid. Whilst the car is being cleaned these chip marks will become evident and it is important that they are attended to immediately, otherwise rusting will occur and start to spread so that what was once a small chip will gradually turn into a large area requiring a great deal more repair work.

Touch-up paint is usually available in a touch-up pencil, a tin with a little brush in the lid, or aerosol form, and may be obtained as a good match to the original body colour. It must, however, be realised that some paint colours are more stable than others. Due to the action of sunlight on an older car, an exact match may be difficult.

Use a touch-up tin with brush incorporated in the lid for making good stone chips and very small scratches.

To prepare the surface for touching-up, first use a silicone solvent to remove all traces of polish which will otherwise not allow the paint to adhere properly. If there are signs of rusting or the paint beginning to lift, use a sharp penknife and carefully scrape away the loose paint and rust. Then neutralise the rust with a little 'Kurust' and allow to dry. With a piece of rag soaked in methylated spirits wipe away the excess.

The prepared spot may now be touched in with the touch-up brush. Very carefully apply a thin coat of paint only to the area concerned and allow to dry thoroughly. Apply a further thin coat of paint so as to build up to the original thickness. This will take time and patience but with care the touch-up should be indistinguishable from the surrounding area.

If there is a scratch on the paintwork which has penetrated the top coat of paint and the red primer is showing the procedure is the same.

The edges of doors and boot lid seem to suffer very much and small areas of rust frequently appear. In this case an aerosol tin of primer and top coat will be required. Again use the silicone solvent to remove any polish from the area concerned. Rub down the paint around the area with a little wet or dry paper grade 400 until the area is smooth. As the name implies, the paper can be used with water without disentegrating. Water flushes the rubber off paint from the abrasive surface of the paper. It would otherwise clog. Neutralise any rust with 'Kurust'. It is useless trying to use an aerosol in damp conditions or in anything other than perfectly still air. So choose a dry day and work in the garage.

Shake the aerosol tin of primer for a few minutes to ensure that there is no sediment in the bottom. Usually the manufacturer drops in a ball bearing to assist agitation of the paint. If this is the first time that an aerosol tin is used, try the spray on a piece of metal such as an old tin to get the 'feel' of it and then proceed to

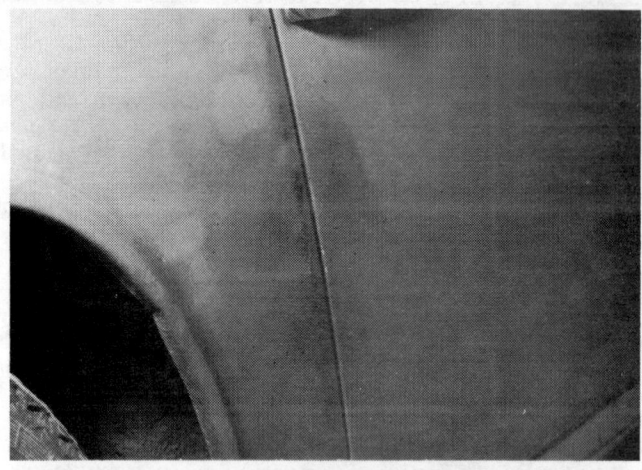

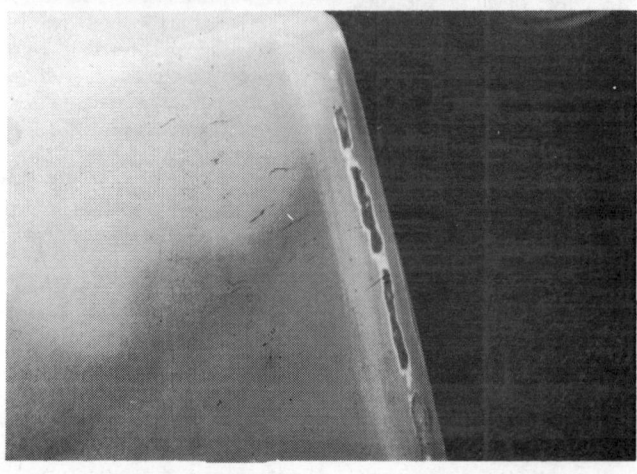

Wing and door edge cleaning ready for painting

spray the prepared surface. Remember the success of this work lies in the preparation. The smoother the prepared surface, the better will be the finish. Hold the jet about 8 - 12 inches away from the area to be sprayed and work from the centre outwards, keeping the centre moist and the outside lightly sprayed and dry.

When dry, lightly rub the primer with wet or dry paper to roughen up the surface and inspect the surface for blemishes caused by dust or insufficient attention being paid at the preparation stage. Rectify any faults found by rubbing down again and applying a further coat of primer. It is only when the surface under repair is perfect that the final top coat may be applied. Again experiment on an old piece of metal if this is your first time and when you are confident apply the top coat to the primer. Remember it is like ordinary household painting - two thin coats are better than one thick coat.

Should runs occur it is an indication that either too much paint has been applied at one go or the nozzle was too near to the surface being sprayed. Rub down the area concerned and start again.

With all touching-up, be it a small spot or a larger area, allow the paint to dry thoroughly, overnight at least, and then use a little rubbing compound to blend in the edges of the paint and remove any dry spray.

If the area is near to a piece of chrome trim there is no need to remove it. Mask up the chrome trim with a little sellotape or proper masking tape. This may be removed once the paint is half dry, leaving no paint overspray marks on the trim. Take care when sticking down the tape and pleat it, if necessary, around any curved areas.

Bodywork - deep scratching, dent or crease removal

This type of repair requires a little more work but is well within the do-it-yourself motorists' capabilities, provided that care is taken and the job is not rushed. Preparation is the secret to good results. The method of approach will depend on the location of the damage, but in all cases if it is possible to push the dent or crease out from behind so much the better. This may mean removal of a piece of trim. Should this present problems do not worry too much provided you are able to build up to the original shape with filler.

For safety reasons this next operation requires a pair of goggles or glasses to protect the eyes. Using an electric sander with an abrasive disc on the rubber pad, remove all the paint right down to the bare metal from the area surrounding the damage as well as the damaged area itself.

Next coat the area of bare metal with a special zinc primer such as 'Galvafroid Zinc Plate' to give additional protection against future corrosion as well as providing a key for the body filler. Allow to dry thoroughly.

The body filler must next be prepared according to the manufacturer's instructions. Usually this comes in two parts, a tin of filler in paste form and a hardener. Read through the mixing instructions and, when fully conversant, mix only enough for immediate use to guard against waste. Once the hardener has been added, the paste has a limited working time of only a few minutes. It is best to mix the material using a piece of plastic or very stiff cardboard on a smooth surface such as a glazed tile.

The filler should be applied to the damaged area and about one inch either side of it so as to allow for preparing the surface for final finishing. Do not apply the filler to paintwork as it will not adhere properly. Carefully smooth the filler to the contour of the body panel, but do not try to work it once it has started to harden.

Make sure that it is left standing proud to give adequate leeway for shaping and rubbing down. When dry, the resin filler has the consistency of a hard bar of chocolate. A 'Surform' plane dreadnought or file and very coarse rasp are ideal articles to use for cutting the material down to the proper contour. As you get nearer to the final shape so the coarseness of the file should be reduced until finally abrasive paper may be used.

Do not use great lumps of filler in one go. Take your time and build up in layers, letting each layer harden in turn. File in uneven spots as and when needed. If you are doing a job using resin paste for the first time do not expect too much of yourself, it takes a little time to get the feel of the material. If an area of panel has rusted out and you have a hole to fill in, then a piece of perforated metal sheet or mesh should be attached behind the panel with adhesive or clips so that the resin filler paste can be built up on it layer by layer.

When you are satisfied that the surface looks

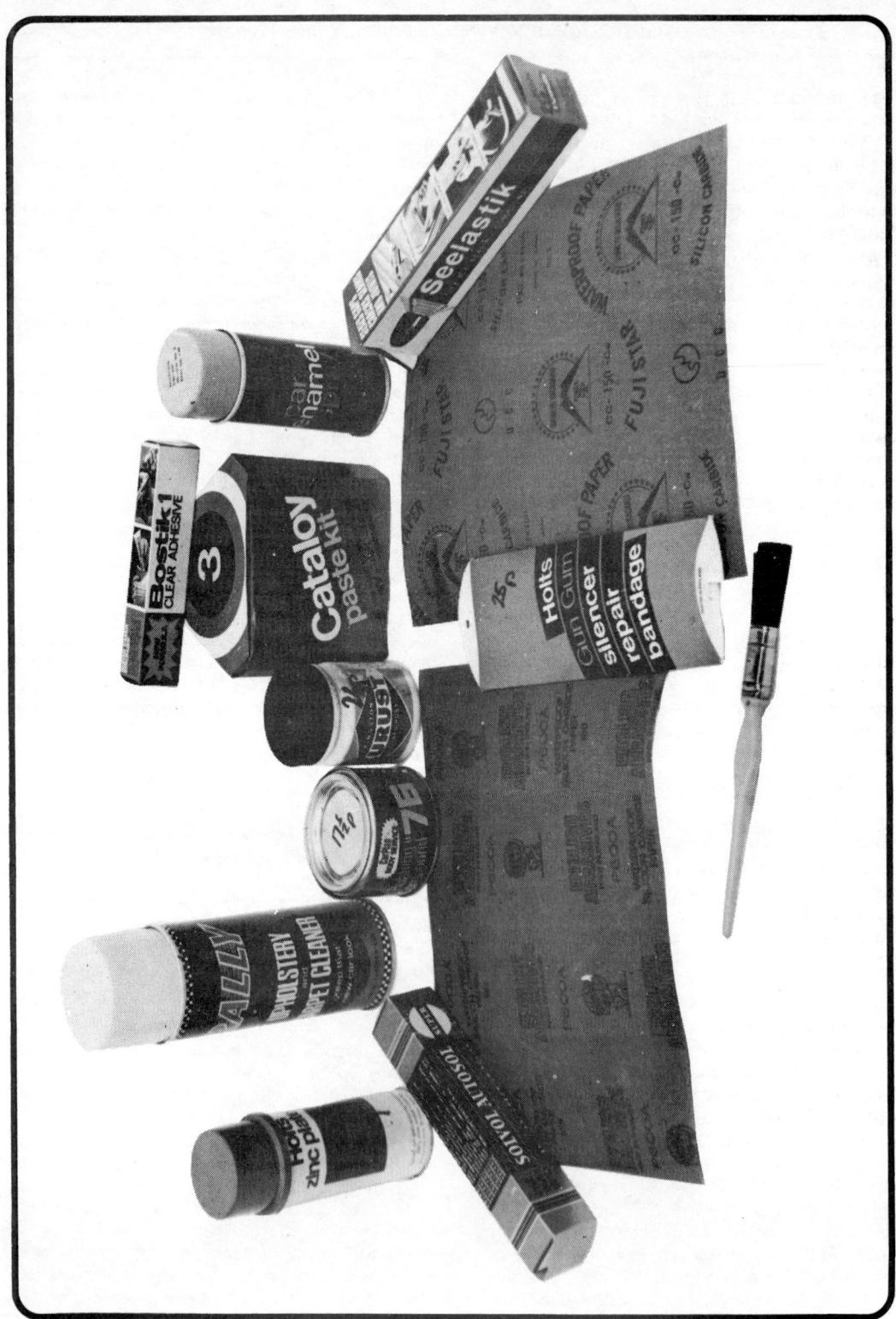

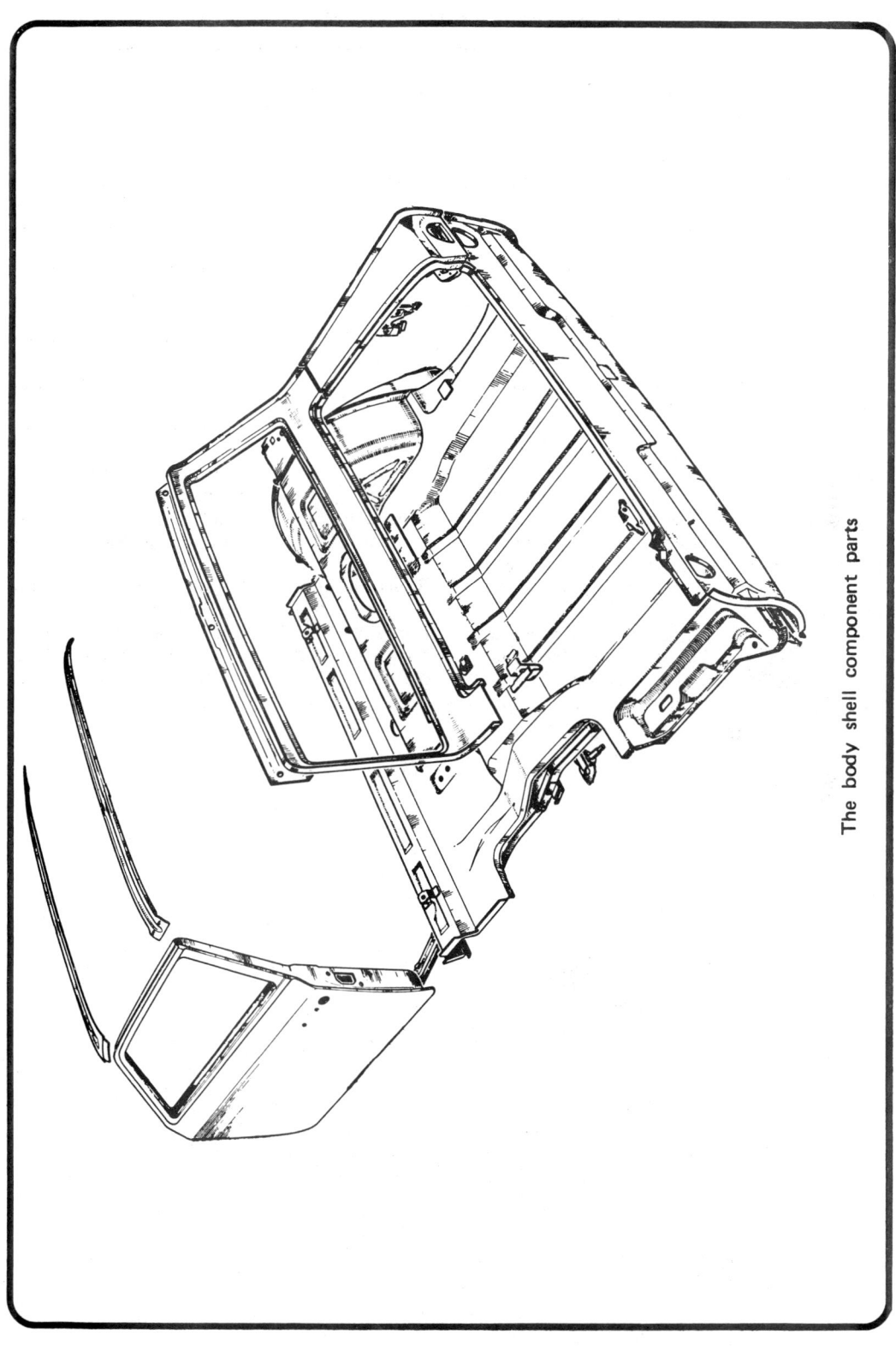

The body shell component parts

and feels even (it does not have to have a glass-like finish yet) apply a coat of cellulose primer (the grey one) to the whole area of filler paste and surround. This can go direct onto bare metal but it is best to cover bare metal with an under primer of 'Galvafroid Zinc Plate' first if possible. This is supplied for brush application or from an aerosol.

After the cellulose primer is dry, it should be rubbed down with 400 wet and dry. Keep adding another coat of primer (after the water has dried off) and rubbing down until a perfectly smooth finish is obtained.

The final colour coat may then be applied from the aerosol can. Do not spray in wind or direct sunlight.

If the area is a large one, it may be worth while to spray the complete panel - which, of course, should be rubbed down all over with 400 grade wet and dry first.

If you have colour sprayed part of a panel only, leave it to harden for at least a fortnight before rubbing down with cutting paste and final polishing.

Provided that care was taken in the selection of the materials, and the instructions followed, the results should be satisfactory but if something has gone wrong the following table should be of assistance:

FAULT	CAUSE
Blotchy finish	Insufficient number of primer or top coats.
Paint runs	Spary nozzle too near panel during spraying. Too much paint applied.
Rippling (called orange peel)	Too thick a coat application
Matt finish	Spray nozzle too far away from panel. Not all dust from previous flatting operation removed.
Creasing	Unsuitable materials used for primer or top coat.
Overspray	Insufficient masking - use cutting compound to remove it.
Rough finish	Spraying in dusty or windy conditions.
Faded patches of top coat (called blooming)	Usually caused by spraying in damp conditions. Most pronounced with dark colours.

Buying and selling a used Viva HA

You may buy a car under one of the following circumstances (other than new which cannot apply of course to an HA series Viva).

1 From an auction
2 From a private individual
3 From a dealer without a garage backing
4 From a garage which also deals in second-hand vehicles

The motor auction calls for some experience and needs a clear cut plan before you go. If you want a Viva then you will have to decide how much you want to pay and then find out what model, year and condition you may expect for this price. If you have a friend 'in the trade' he can give you a fair idea of current prices. If not, buy a copy of the 'Motorist's Guide' which appears monthly. It is the best indication of buying prices for all types of secondhand cars. 'Glass's Guide' to used car prices is not available to people other than accredited dealers so the author of this handbook, who is not a car dealer, can only say that the difference between the buying and selling price of any car is around 20 per cent.

Auction buying can be very time consuming and frustrating - particularly as one does not know whether the car will be sold at all - the reserve price may not be reached. So if you are specifically buying a Viva it is advisable not to expect too much joy from an auction.

When buying from a private individual you may expect to buy for a lower price than from a dealer. Much also depends on the reasons for which the individual is selling. If he wishes to buy another car he would normally obtain the best sale terms by trading his car in. On the other hand he may be short of cash, so put yourself in his position before driving too hard a bargain.

However, depending on what terms you buy the car, remember that any redress for faults which occur later will be much more difficult to obtain from a private transaction.

If you buy a car from a dealer who has no garage servicing or repair organisation directly associated with him, you are likely to find difficulty if cause of dissatisfaction occurs. Although you would be protected, if he is a bona fide dealer, much fuss and delay is likely to result if a garage has to be called in independently to deal with faults or repairs.

The fourth alternative, to buy a used car from a garage, is the one which most people go for. If the garage is near where you live, so much the better. Reputations of garages vary but if troubles do develop it is well worth considering the relative costs and convenience of dealing with a garage two miles or ten miles away.

Having considered the places to buy, the next thing to consider is the car itself.

Here you must decide on one of two approaches. Will you inspect it (alone or with perhaps a knowledgeable friend) or pay a few pounds to a motoring organisation to inspect it for you first? If the seller agrees to an independent inspection this is a good sign but you must appreciate that if he sells it to someone else before you can get the inspection carried out (or even before the inspection is completed) you have no come-back unless you pay a deposit. If the dealer will not agree to an independent inspection from a motoring organisation it usually means that the seller has not thoroughly examined the vehicle and does not know what may be wrong or is trying to hide something. It is more usual for the older model, cheaper bargains, to fall into this category. If the seller does not cooperate for an independent inspection on a later model, top price car, be very wary indeed.

If you intend to have an independent inspection carried out then it is assumed that the general visible state of the car is good. You should also carry out Section 1 of the checks in the 'Owner/Inspection' guide given later. This is to avoid wasting time and money in case any of the basic requirements cannot be fulfilled.

Body parts prone to rusting on the Viva HA

Buyers 'Owner/Inspection' Guide

Section 1 Preliminaries
1 Ask to see the registration book. If not immediately available ask why and be suspicious if reasons given are vague. Check the number of previous owners. If more than an average of one per year this is an adverse point.
2 Ask to see the MOT certificate. If near expiry ask why it has not been renewed. If no reason given then do not buy until the test has been carried out - at the seller's expense.
3 Examine the tyres on both sides to check for condition and uniformity of type (radial or cross-ply). If there should be a mixture of radial and cross-ply the only permissible arrangement is with the two radials on the rear wheels. Do not be driven in, or drive, the car if there is any other mixture.
4 Examine the bodywork inside and out and note, but do not comment on at this stage, any particularly obvious marks or damage. Look into the engine compartment. If very clean - good. If not grimace for the seller's benefit and close the bonnet quickly. Make sure you have comprehensive insurance before asking to drive the car yourself.

Section 2 Test Drive
1 It is normal for the seller to drive the car at first with you as passenger. If otherwise, he should accompany you. An unscrupulous person could accuse you of damaging the car in some way if you go off alone.
2 As a passenger, note how the engine starts and the general operational smoothness of the controls. Make allowance for the fact that the seller may be a salesman who is not over-familiar with the particular car. A car driven by a private owner will usually seem to perform very smoothly as he will be familiar with any of its idiosyncrasies.
3 Make every effort to get out of a limited speed zone and ask the driver to get up to a speed of at least 60 mph. Keep an ear open for howling transmission or excessive body drumming. Early Vivas had an unhappy reputation in this area and you should know about it.
4 When driving the car yourself first note that the engine starts without fuss. Gear engagement should be achieved without noise. (If you have never driven a Viva the gear lever positions may strike you as unusual at first).
5 Before moving off, leave the handbrake on and let the clutch in slowly. If the car moves

the handbrake needs adjustment. If the clutch comes on a long way (or all the way) without the car moving it needs overhauling which is a moderately expensive job.
6 When moving off power-take-up should be smooth and noise free. Gear changing should be smooth and quiet.
7 Try the brakes gently to 'feel' their power and note the distance the pedal has to move before the brakes start to work. A lot of movement may simply mean the need for adjustment but the brake linings may be getting close to needing renewal. If the brakes feel spongy, uneven or inefficient, stop the car and ask the seller to drive back.
8 When you are satisfied that the brakes respond correctly, increase speed and assure yourself that the steering feels right. If it is not light and precise, but judders and wanders, stop the car and let the seller drive back.
9 Brakes and steering being satisfactory, ask whether you may increase speed to at least 60 mph (road conditions permitting). Any wandering in the steering or vibrations which now occur may mean that wear has occurred in certain areas which cannot be detected at lower speeds. When braking from the higher speeds 'dab' the brakes and decide whether there is any fore and aft pitching movement of the car. Such a condition may also occur on uneven road surfaces and indicates that the suspension dampers may be faulty.
10 If the seller should talk excessively about the car, other than in direct answer to any questions you ask, it may indicate that he wants to fend-off any questions. If therefore you have some questions you want to ask cut in firmly and ask them. Disregard what he may be rambling on about.

Section 3 Static Examination
1 If everything has proceeded favourably so far do not react with too much enthusiasm. Do not let the salesman lead you away from the car when you have returned to the garage. Open the bonnet once more. If that engine was originally very clean see that it still is. Query any signs of oil or water leakage that may have occurred.
2 If you are at a garage ask whether the vehicle may be put on a lift, hoist or run over a pit. You want to look underneath, so why get dirty? If the seller shows signs of impatience at this just say firmly that you intend to look underneath anyway (you are presumably genuinely interested in buying by now) and do not

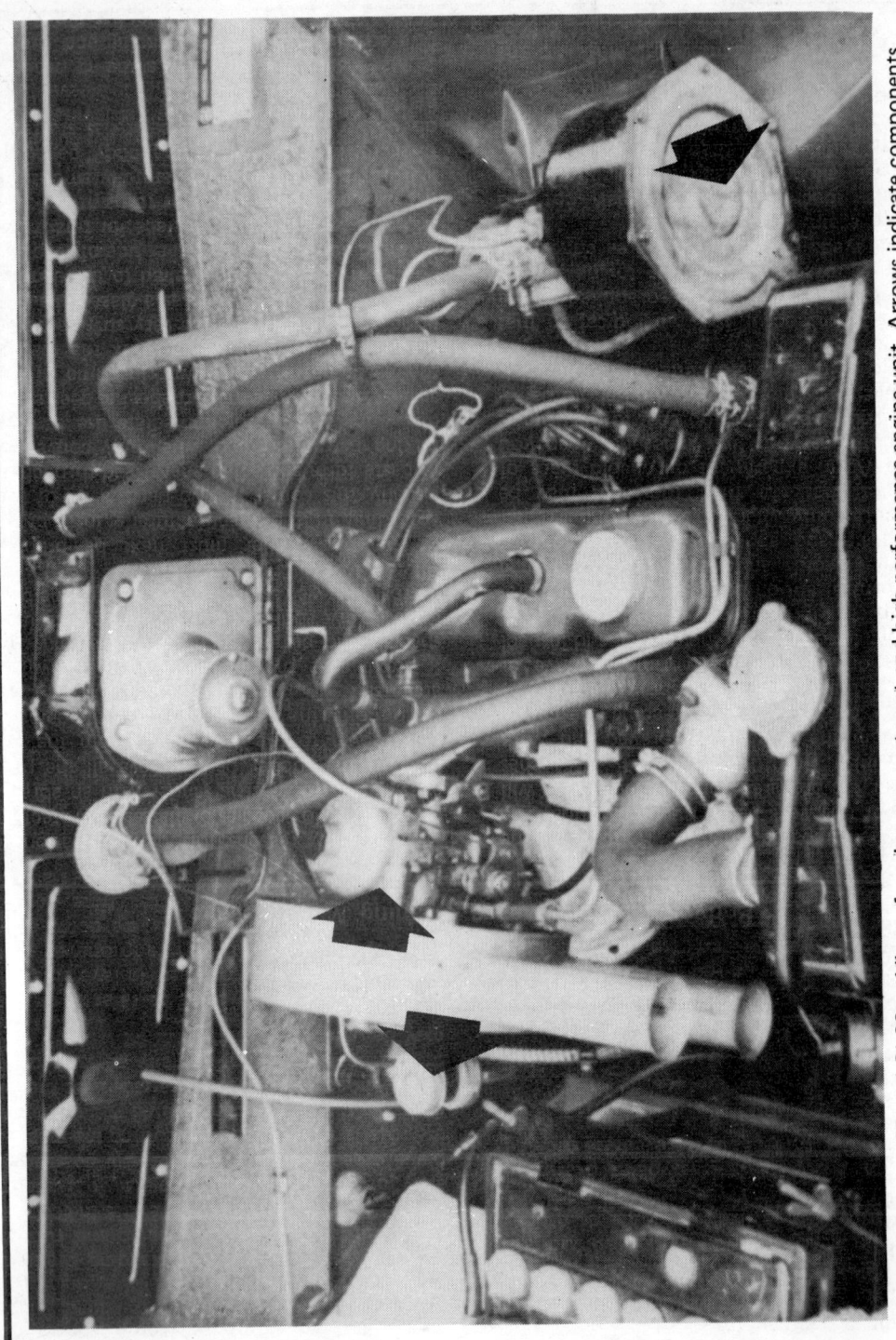

Viva De Luxe 90 and SL90 — View of engine compartment and high performance engine unit. Arrows indicate components which differ from the standard models

intend grovelling around when it is not necessary. Say you can come back in an hour if it will suit him and then go and have a cup of tea somewhere. He will soon arrange for you to inspect the car. If he sees you are genuinely interested and a prospective customer he will not want to let you out of his grasp! You must take advantage of this and make sure that all your reasonable requests are attended to. If you are dealing with a private owner with no facilities you should have provided for the need to get underneath by wearing old clothes or bringing overalls along. It is possible to see most of the car underneath without jacking it up but make the most of any humps or kerbs to position the car for the most advantageous access.

3 If there were indications of steering wander during the driving test examine the steering and front wheel bearings as described under the maintenance schedule 'S' (safety check).

4 Look at the inside walls of the tyres for signs of cuts or fractures that may not have been noticed in the initial 'once over'.

5 Examine the exhaust system for signs of leaks, holes or welds and see that the support brackets are in good order. Exhaust systems rarely last more than two years. Even if there is one small hole anywhere it usually indicates that the whole lot will need renewal very soon.

6 Examine the floor panels for dents and rust. Rust which has obviously become well established will need attention without delay. The sill panels under the doors are vulnerable to throwback from the front wheels and this is particularly prevalent where front wing mudflaps are not fitted.

7 If there were any 'clunking' noises in the transmission during the driving test they will have been caused by the propeller shaft universal joints or the back axle differential assembly. If it is only the universal joints the repair job is not too costly. To test the universals, grasp the flange on one side of the joint and the shaft on the other and see if there is any movement between the two halves. There should be none. If the universal joints are satisfactory, then the noise must come from somewhere such as the rear axle or gearbox. These are costly repair items. Signs of oil thrown out at the points where the propeller shaft joins both the rear axle and the gearbox indicate that an oil seal has worn out. This in turn means that the rear axle and/or the gearbox may have run for some time with insufficient oil, thus causing

excessive wear. If the areas at both ends of the propshaft are extraordinarily clean it may mean that oil thrown out has been carefully wiped away.

8 Examine the suspension shock absorbers for any signs of oil leaking from them. If there is any such sign then they will need renewal sooner or later, depending on whether they are still effectively damping the up-and-down rebound of the springs.

9 Having finished underneath, wash your hands and dust yourself off and then finally sit in the back seat of the car and look around. Check on carpets, roof lining, upholstery (wear, cracks and tears) window sills and surrounds (rust, leaks, weatherstrips) and door apertures (rust and draught excluders). Check that all the accessories and equipment function (windscreen wipers, heater, etc as fitted).

10 Finally check that the doors shut easily, squarely and without having to slam them. If there should be difficulty in closing them see whether they fit the apertures correctly. If they are out of alignment it could mean one of two things - either the doors have been strained or the bodywork is twisted. This is serious. A twisted body shell could account for any unusual steering behaviour that could not be explained with mechanical components.

11 Take another look at the paintwork to satisfy yourself that it is now no worse than it may have seemed originally. If it is very good on an early model the car may have been resprayed. This is all right provided it is not hiding any crash damage repairs. Take another close look! Use a magnet to test suspect areas for having been filled up with resin filler compound. Filler is acceptable but not in excess.

Section 4 Decision

1 If you are assessing a car from a large reputable firm the main problem will be the price they are asking. Consider the guarantees you should have before condeming them too roundly! They are not likely to get involved in bargaining but you could ask if they will accept an offer (this is not likely if you seek HP terms). If they say they may consider it, offer 10% less than their asking price. You may end up with 5% off.

2 If you hope to buy from a less secure source, such as a small or part-time dealer or a private owner, signs of imminent mechanical repair needs or poor bodywork may call for a drastic price reduction. You can often get the car for

20% less if you wave money under the man's nose.

3 If you are a keen do-it-yourself 'car man' you may get a bargain because you can assess what it will cost additionally to put the vehicle in good shape. For those who seek only reliability and cannot afford time for other than simple maintenance and repair tasks, the best guarantee conditions are the most important thing, vis-a-vis price and proximity of the garage.

Selling

Much or what has been said with regard to buying a used Viva HA is relevant to selling one, except, of course, that the boot is on the other foot.

Whatever the reasons are for selling, be they that you want a bigger, better or different car; you simply need the money; or your circumstances have changed; there is one common factor: you want the best price for it.

Do not sell it to a relative or friend unless he offers to take it from you. Even then you should discuss and if he knows what you are asking knock off a tenner.

Do not try and put one over on a private buyer either - you will not get much satisfaction from it. If you put one over on a dealer you are to be congratulated!

Whoever you hope to buy from you, there is a basic preparation: cleanliness is all. The cleaner the car, the higher the price. The bodywork's condition, both inside and out, should be the main selling point. Mechanical repair work is usually cheaper and faster to undertake than extensive bodywork repairs or renovation. The condition of the bodywork is usually indicative of the total condition of the car because it will show signs of age and disrepair sooner than the engine or gearbox, particularly on cars more than three years old. It is unlikely that an owner will keep a car in excellent condition mechanically and allow the body to drop off around it. Attend to the paintwork, chrome and all exterior trim, clean the outside thoroughly and polish the car, clean out the boot, the engine compartment and 'spring clean' the interior. There are methods of doing this explained in the Bodywork Chapter of this book. As a buyer you will know the importance of the first visual impression.

As there are various ways of buying a used car, so there are similar methods of selling, but they are considered on their merits from completely different standpoints. The way in which you sell your car will depend on why you are selling. The best prices are often obtained when part exchanging your car for a new one from an accredited dealer. However, shop around from dealer to dealer; their buying-in prices will vary according to how eager they are to sell the new car you want, and how eager they are to actually have your present car to resell. Nevertheless, with many dealers not wanting used cars of more than three years old it may be better to sell privately whatever your circumstances. Here, local papers, notice boards etc are the best media for selling.

It is unlikely that you will receive the best price from a used car dealer at least as a cash transaction, unless he requires a good example for a particular customer, because he will have to put his mark-up onto the car to resell. Auctions do not often provide the best recompense. You can, of course, put on a reserve price. They usually do provide a sale at a low price if you are finding it difficult to sell your particular car.

The same premise applies when you are selling your car as when you are buying one, with regard to the actual selling price. The same guide is valid. However, there are other indications. Go around to various dealers and ask them for the prices of used cars of a similar age and condition to yours and look at the prices in the local papers, and then fix a reasonable price and be prepared to bargain. There are obviously price trends with regard to time and place to sell. Prices usually creep upwards in the spring and you may be fortunate enough to live in a high demand area such as London or Eastern England where prices will again be marginally higher than elsewhere.

In conclusion remember when selling your car that the law exists both to protect you and the buyer. The Trades Description Act does affect you as the seller. If the car you are selling is under a hire purchase agreement, the permission of the finance company must be obtained first. Irrespective of the age of your car it must have a current road fund licence, MOT certificate (when applicable) and insurance before it can even be tested on the road. Always give a receipt and do not part with the car and log book until you are sure you have the money, if you are paid by cheque. Do not forget to make sure your name is removed from the log book and the buyer's inserted and that the local Taxation Office is informed of a change of ownership.

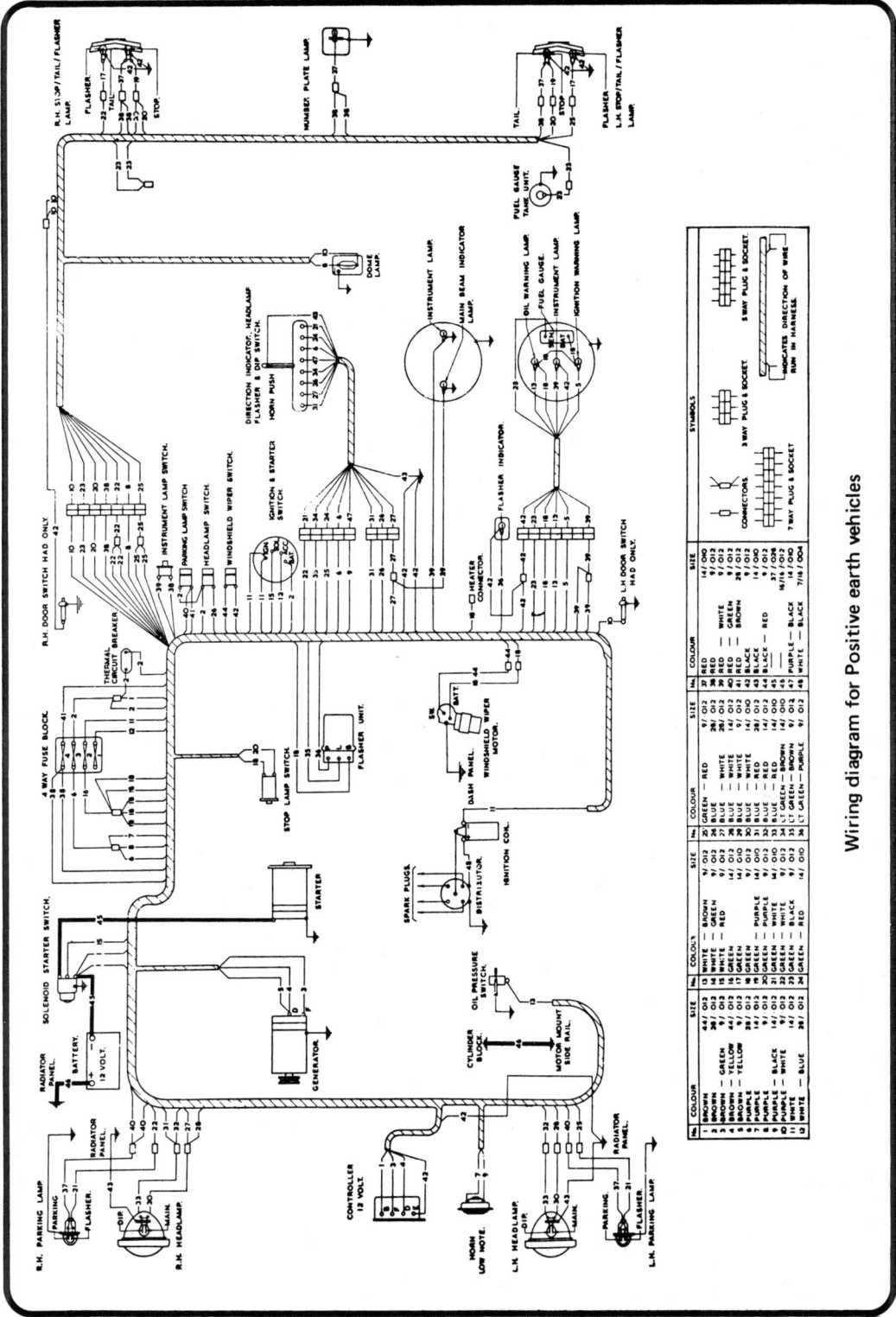

Wiring diagram for Positive earth vehicles

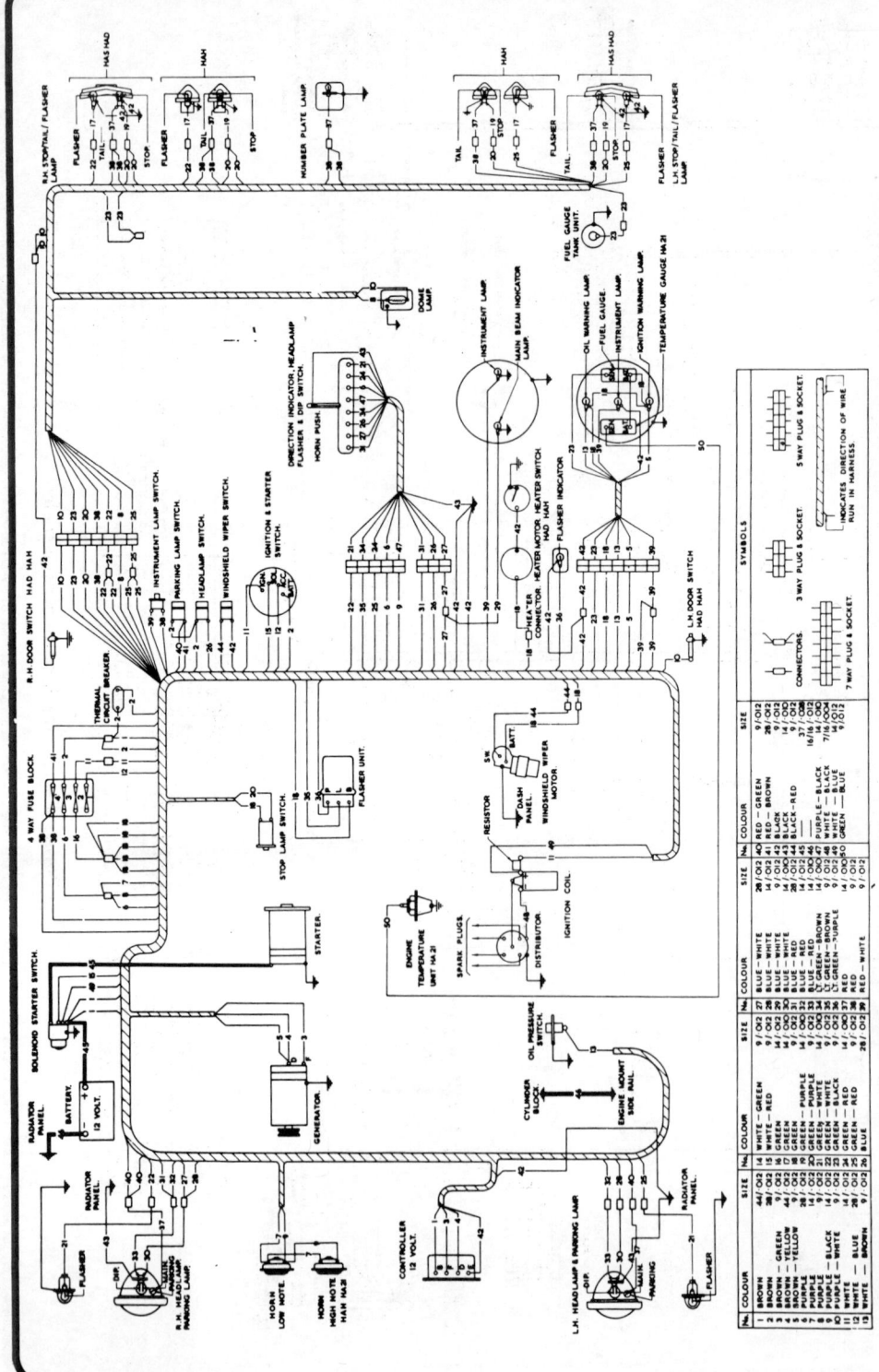

Wiring diagram for Negative earth vehicles (incorporating circuits for combined head/parking light, heater motor and low ambient temperature ignition coil)

Castrol GRADES

Castrol Engine Oils

Castrol GTX

An ultra high performance SAE 20W/50 motor oil which exceeds the latest API MS requirements and manufacturers' specifications. Castrol GTX with liquid tungsten† generously protects engines at the extreme limits of performance, and combines both good cold starting with oil consumption control. Approved by leading car makers.

Castrol XL 20/50

Contains liquid tungsten†; well suited to the majority of conditions giving good oil consumption control in both new and old cars.

Castrolite (Multi-grade)

This is the lightest multi-grade oil of the Castrol motor oil family containing liquid tungsten†. It is best suited to ensure easy winter starting and for those car models whose manufacturers specify lighter weight oils.

Castrol Grand Prix

An SAE 50 engine oil for use where a heavy, full-bodied lubricant is required.

Castrol Two-Stroke-Four

A premium SAE 30 motor oil possessing good detergency characteristics and corrosion inhibitors, coupled with low ash forming tendency and excellent anti-scuff properties. It is suitable for all two-stroke motor-cycles, and for two-stroke and small four-stroke horticultural machines.

Castrol CR (Multi-grade)

A high quality engine oil of the SAE-20W/30 multi-grade type, suited to mixed fleet operations.

Castrol CRI 10, 20, 30

Primarily for diesel engines, a range of heavily fortified, fully detergent oils, covering the requirements of DEF 2101-D and Supplement 1 specifications.

Castrol CRB 20, 30

Primarily for diesel engines, heavily fortified, fully detergent oils, covering the requirements of MIL-L-2104B.

Castrol R 40

Primarily designed and developed for highly stressed racing engines. Castrol 'R' should not be mixed with any other oil nor with any grade of Castrol.

†Liquid Tungsten is an oil soluble long chain tertiary alkyl primary amine tungstate covered by British Patent No. 882,295.

Castrol Gear Oils

Castrol Hypoy (90 EP)

A light-bodied powerful extreme pressure gear oil for use in hypoid rear axles and in some gearboxes.

Castrol Gear Oils (continued)

Castrol Hypoy Light (80 EP)

A very light-bodied powerful extreme pressure gear oil for use in hypoid rear axles in cold climates and in some gearboxes.

Castrol Hypoy B (90 EP)

A light-bodied powerful extreme pressure gear oil that complies with the requirements of the MIL-L-2105B specification, for use in certain gearboxes and rear axles.

Castrol Hi-Press (140 EP)

A heavy-bodied extreme pressure gear oil for use in spiral bevel rear axles and some gearboxes.

Castrol ST (90)

A light-bodied gear oil with fortifying additives

Castrol D (140)

A heavy full-bodied gear oil with fortifying additives.

Castrol Thio-Hypoy FD (90 EP)

A light-bodied powerful extreme pressure gear oil. This is a special oil for running-in certain hypoid gears.

Automatic Transmission Fluids

Castrol TQF
(Automatic Transmission Fluid)

Approved for use in all Borg-Warner Automatic Transmission Units. Castrol TQF also meets Ford specification M2C 33F.

Castrol TQ Dexron®
(Automatic Transmission Fluid)

Complies with the requirements of Dexron® Automatic Transmission Fluids as laid down by General Motors Corporation.

Castrol Greases

Castrol LM

A multi-purpose high melting point lithium based grease approved for most automotive applications including chassis and wheel bearing lubrication.

Castrol MS3

A high melting point lithium based grease containing molybdenum disulphide.

Castrol BNS

A high melting point grease for use where recommended by certain manufacturers in front wheel bearings when disc brakes are fitted.

Castrol Greases (continued)

Castrol CL

A semi-fluid calcium based grease, which is both waterproof and adhesive, intended for chassis lubrication.

Castrol Medium

A medium consistency calcium based grease.

Castrol Heavy

A heavy consistency calcium based grease.

Castrol PH

A white grease for plunger housings and other moving parts on brake mechanisms. *It must NOT be allowed to come into contact with brake fluid when applied to the moving parts of hydraulic brakes.*

Castrol Graphited Grease

A graphited grease for the lubrication of transmission chains.

Castrol Under-Water Grease

A grease for the under-water gears of outboard motors.

Anti-Freeze

Castrol Anti-Freeze

Contains anti-corrosion additives with ethylene glycol. Recommended for the cooling systems of all petrol and diesel engines.

Speciality Products

Castrol Girling Damper Oil Thin

The oil for Girling piston type hydraulic dampers.

Castrol Shockol

A light viscosity oil for use in some piston type shock absorbers and in some hydraulic systems employing synthetic rubber seals. It must not be used in braking systems.

Castrol Penetrating Oil

A leaf spring lubricant possessing a high degree of penetration and providing protection against rust.

Castrol Solvent Flushing Oil

A light-bodied solvent oil, designed for flushing engines, rear axles, gearboxes and gearcasings.

Castrollo

An upper cylinder lubricant for use in the proportion of 1 fluid ounce to two gallons of fuel.

Everyman Oil

A light-bodied machine oil containing anti-corrosion additives for both general use and cycle lubrication.

Metric Conversion Tables

Inches	Millimetres	Inches	Millimetres
0.001	0.0254	0.1	2.54
0.002	0.0508	0.2	5.08
0.003	0.0762	0.3	7.62
0.004	0.1016	0.4	10.16
0.005	0.1270	0.5	12.70
0.006	0.1524	0.6	15.24
0.007	0.1778	0.7	17.78
0.008	0.2032	0.8	20.32
0.009	0.2286	0.9	22.96
0.01	0.254	1.0	25.4
0.02	0.508	2.0	50.8
0.03	0.762	3.0	76.2
0.04	1.016	4.0	101.6
0.05	1.270	5.0	127.0
0.06	1.524	6.0	152.4
0.07	1.778	7.0	177.8
0.08	2.032	8.0	203.2
0.09	2.286	9.0	228.6
		10.0	254.0

Torque Wrench Settings

lb ft	Kg m	Kg m	lb ft
1	0.138	1	7.233
2	0.276	2	14.466
3	0.414	3	21.699
4	0.553	4	28.932
5	0.691	5	36.165
6	0.829	6	43.398
7	0.967	7	50.631
8	1.106	8	57.864
9	1.244	9	65.097
10	1.382	10	72.330
20	2.765	20	144.660
30	4.147	30	216.990

Metric Conversion Table

Distance

Miles	Kilometres	Kilometres	Miles
1	1.61	1	0.62
2	3.22	2	1.24
3	4.83	3	1.86
4	6.44	4	2.49
5	8.05	5	3.11
6	9.66	6	3.73
7	11.27	7	4.35
8	12.88	8	4.97
9	14.48	9	5.59
10	16.09	10	6.21
20	32.19	20	12.43
30	48.28	30	18.64
40	64.37	40	24.85
50	80.47	50	31.07
60	96.56	60	37.28
70	112.65	70	43.50
80	128.75	80	49.71
90	144.84	90	55.92
100	160.93	100	62.14

Capacities

Pints	Litres	Litres	Pints	Gallons	Litres	Litres	Gallons
1	0.57	1	1.76	1	4.55	1	0.22
2	1.14	2	3.52	2	0.09	2	0.44
3	1.70	3	5.28	3	13.64	3	0.66
4	2.27	4	7.04	4	18.18	4	0.88
5	2.84	5	8.80	5	22.73	5	1.10
6	3.41	6	10.56	6	27.28	6	1.32
7	3.98	7	12.32	7	31.82	7	1.54
8	4.55	8	14.08	8	36.37	8	1.76
9	5.11	9	15.841	9	40.91	9	1.98
10	5.58	10	17.60	10	45.46	10	2.20
11	6.25	11	19.36	11	50.01	20	4.40
12	6.82	12	21.12	12	54.56	30	6.60

Metric Conversion Table

Tyre Pressures

lb/sq in	Kg/sq cm	Kg/sq cm	lb/sq in
1	0.07	1	14.22
2	0.14	2	28.50
3	0.21	3	42.67
4	0.28	4	56.89
5	0.35	5	71.12
6	0.42	6	85.34
7	0.49	7	99.56
8	0.56	8	113.79
9	0.63	9	128.00
10	0.70	10	142.23
20	1.41	20	284.47
30	2.11	30	426.70

Inches	Decimals	Millimetres
$1/64$	0.0156	0.3969
$1/32$	0.0313	0.7937
$1/16$	0.0625	1.5875
$1/8$	0.125	3.1750
$3/16$	0.1875	4.7625
$1/4$	0.25	6.3500
$5/16$	0.3125	7.9375
$3/8$	0.375	9.5250
$7/16$	0.4375	11.1125
$1/2$	0.5	12.7000
$9/16$	0.5625	14.2875
$5/8$	0.625	15.8750
$11/16$	0.6875	17.4625
$3/4$	0.75	19.0500
$13/16$	0.8125	20.6375
$7/8$	0.875	22.2250
$15/16$	0.9375	23.8125

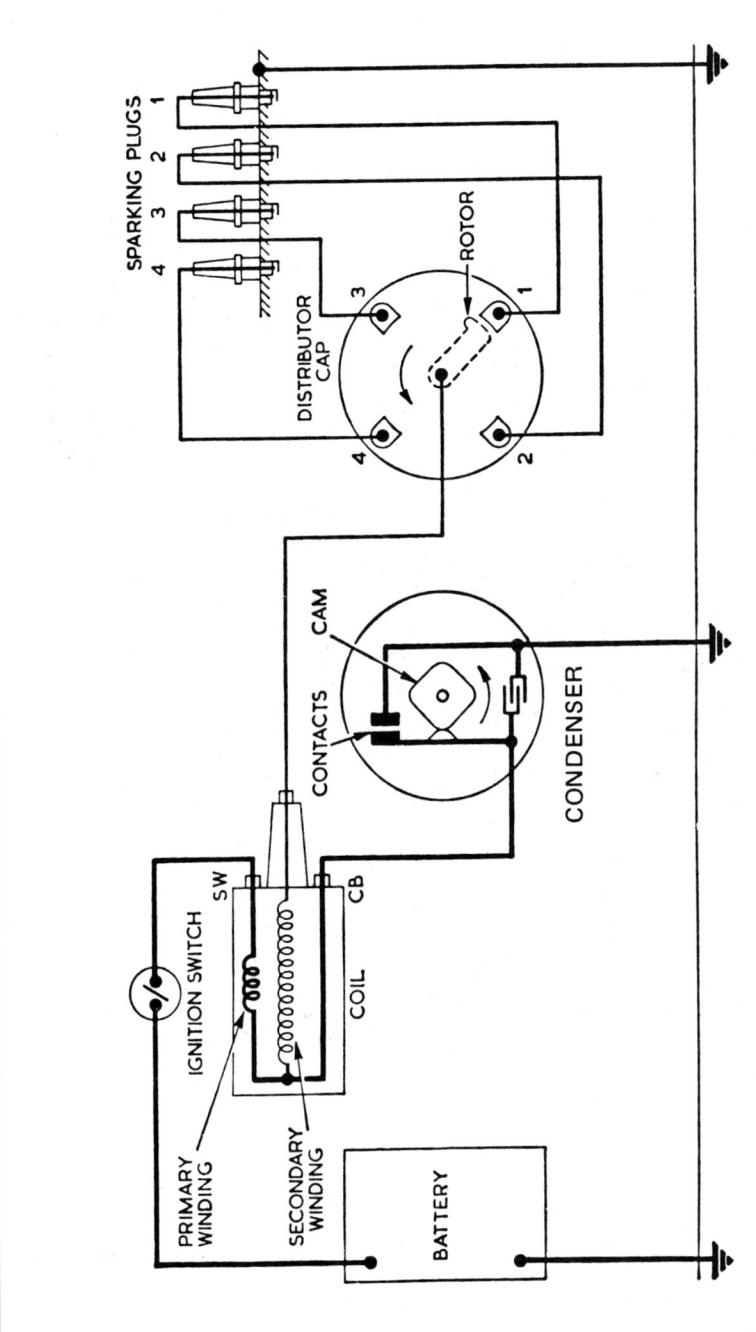

The ignition circuit - LT system indicated by heavier lines

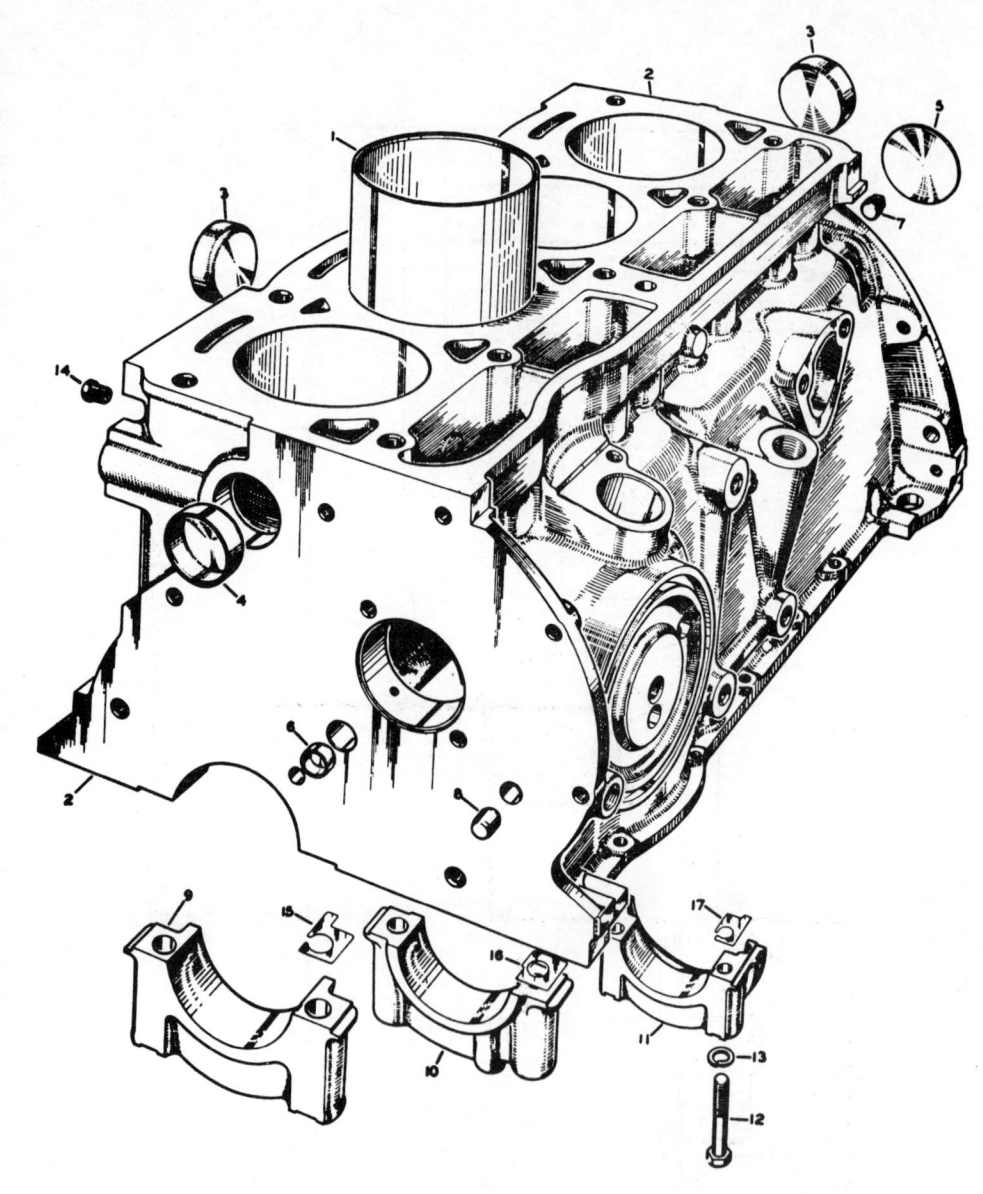

Cylinder block components

1	Cylinder liner	7	Plug, oil gallery	13	Cap, bolt and washer
2	Block and crankcase	8	Plug, oil hole	14	Plug - drain hole
3	Plug - (cooling water gallery)	9	Crankshaft bearing cap - front	15	Cap shims
4	Plug - (cooling water gallery)	10	Crankshaft bearing cap - centre	16	Cap shims
5	Plug - camshaft	11	Crankshaft bearing cap - rear	17	Cap shims
6	Plug - oil gallery	12	Cap, bolt and washer		

Fault finding chart

How to use the Fault Finding Charts

The fault finding charts have been specially written to help the Viva HA owner remedy certain situations which he may find himself in. We have imagined the driver sitting in the car faced with situations, such as the car will just not start in the morning or the steering starts to wander, and needing help. A logical step-by-step progression is made suggesting symptoms, then possible faults and a remedy. It has been our intention to try to get the car going if stopped or for the driver to keep motoring at least in knowledge of the fault which may be worrying him. We have re-stated how remedying tasks are done in many cases but we do assume that the driver has actually read the 'Routine Maintenance' Chapter in his handbook and refer him to it in the less frustrating sections. Do not hesitate to turn from section to section to find the possible symptom straight away without always wading through from the beginning. Each section within a section is complete in itself.

THE CAR WILL NOT START OR STOPS ON THE ROAD AND WILL NOT RE-START
Battery, starter motor, ignition and carburation check

EMERGENCY
Brakes inoperative, steering poor, clutch not working, and lights

FAULTS AND DIFFICULTIES
Engine and associated features - generator malfunctioning, overheating and loss of power
Other features - gearbox, clutch and noises

The car will not start or stops on the road and will not re-start

Symptom Ignition warning light fails to come on when ignition switched on

Possible Fault	Check and Remedy
Battery flat or leads loose. Ignition warning light faulty	Check to see if headlights work. If not, clean and tighten down battery leads and check to see if lights then function and ignition warning light is on. If no lights, battery flat, recharge or replace.

Symptom Ignition warning light on but starter fails to turn engine

Possible Fault	Check and Remedy
Battery flat or battery and starter lead connections are dirty or loose	Check intensity of headlights. If dim, battery needs charging. Car can be push or tow started (not automatic). If lights are bright check all battery, solenoid and starter motor leads for corrosion, cleanliness and tightness.
Starter motor jammed	Turn the square head of the starter motor shaft with a spanner to free it, or place the car in a high gear and rock it to and fro to free the drive pinion from the flywheel teeth.

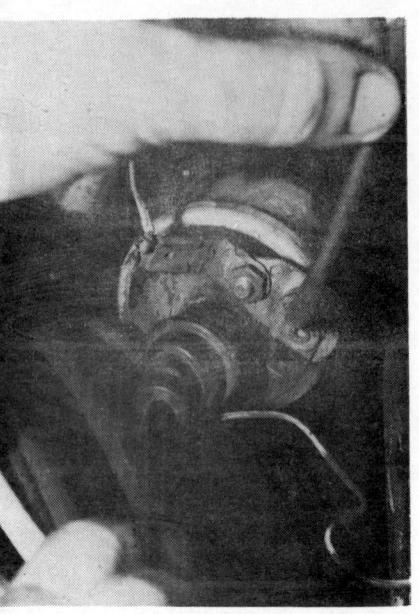

Faulty LT leads at the coil

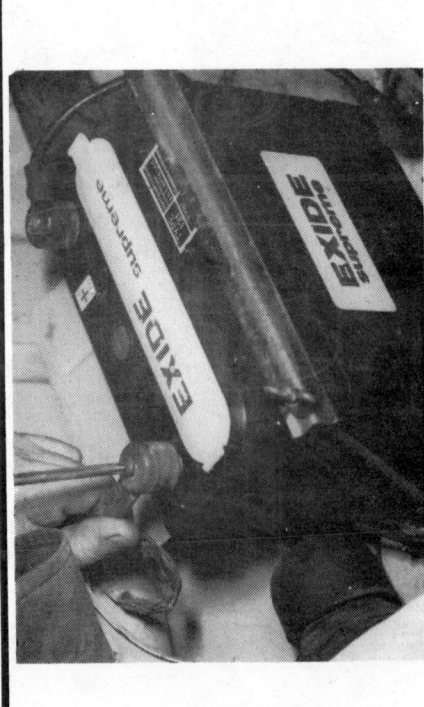

Loose battery terminals

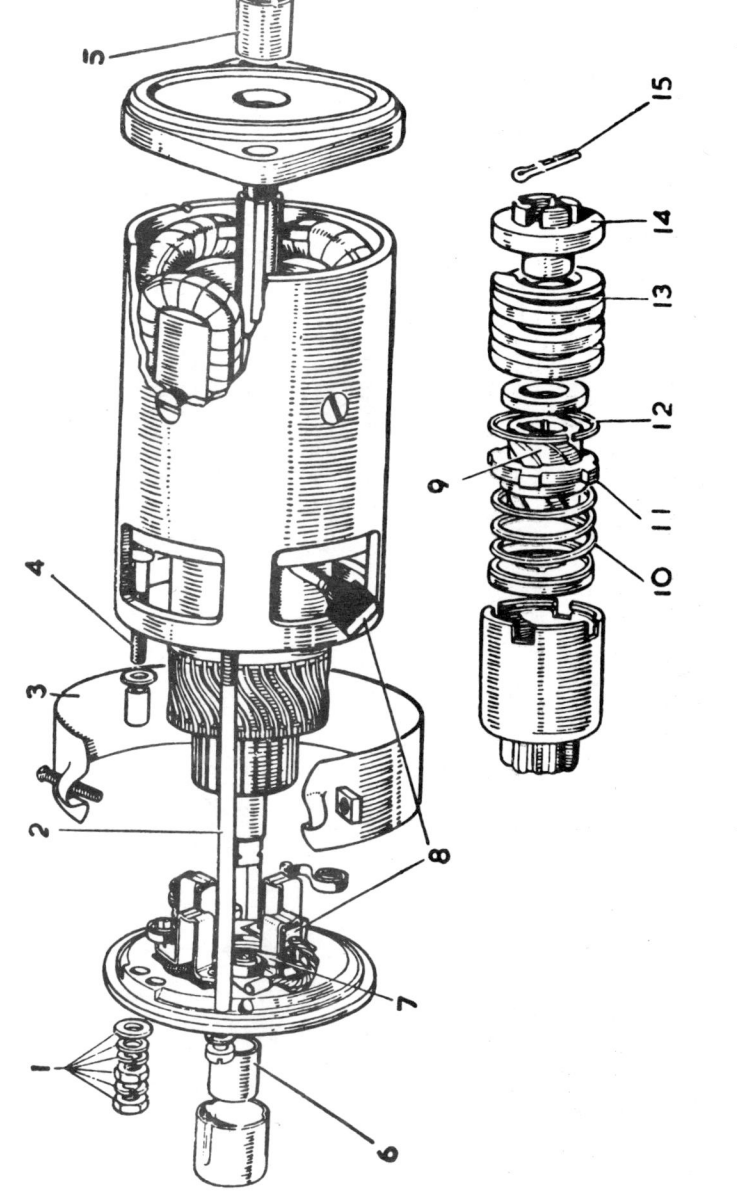

The starter motor and drive

1 Terminal nuts & washers
2 Through bolt
3 Cover band
4 Terminal post

5 Bearing bush
6 Bearing bush
7 Brush spring
8 Brushes

9 Sleeve
10 Restraining spring
11 Control nut
12 Retaining ring

13 Main spring
14 Shaft nut
15 Cotter pin

The car will not start or stops on the road and will not re-start

Possible Fault	Check and Remedy
Defective solenoid switch	Bridge the main terminal of the solenoid switch with a large screwdriver blade or piece of heavy duty cable. Do not worry about sparks but keep fingers clear of contact points which will get hot. If the starter motor functions the solenoid is defective and must be replaced. The car can be push started.
Starter motor defective	If all the above methods fail to produce a result the starter motor is defective and must be removed and repaired or renewed. However, the car can still push or tow started.

Symptom Starter turns engine over slowly but with insufficient power to start it

Possible Fault	Check and Remedy
Battery flat or battery and starter lead connections are dirty or loose	Check battery, solenoid and starter motor leads for dirt, corrosion and tightness. If no improvement charge battery. Car can be push or tow started. If the battery fails to hold its charge under normal working conditions have the battery itself checked. If the battery is in good condition have the charging system similarly checked. If in bad condition replace the battery.

Faulty starter solenoid switch

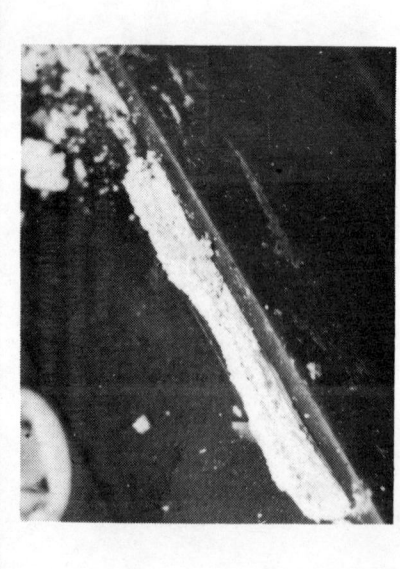

Corroded battery

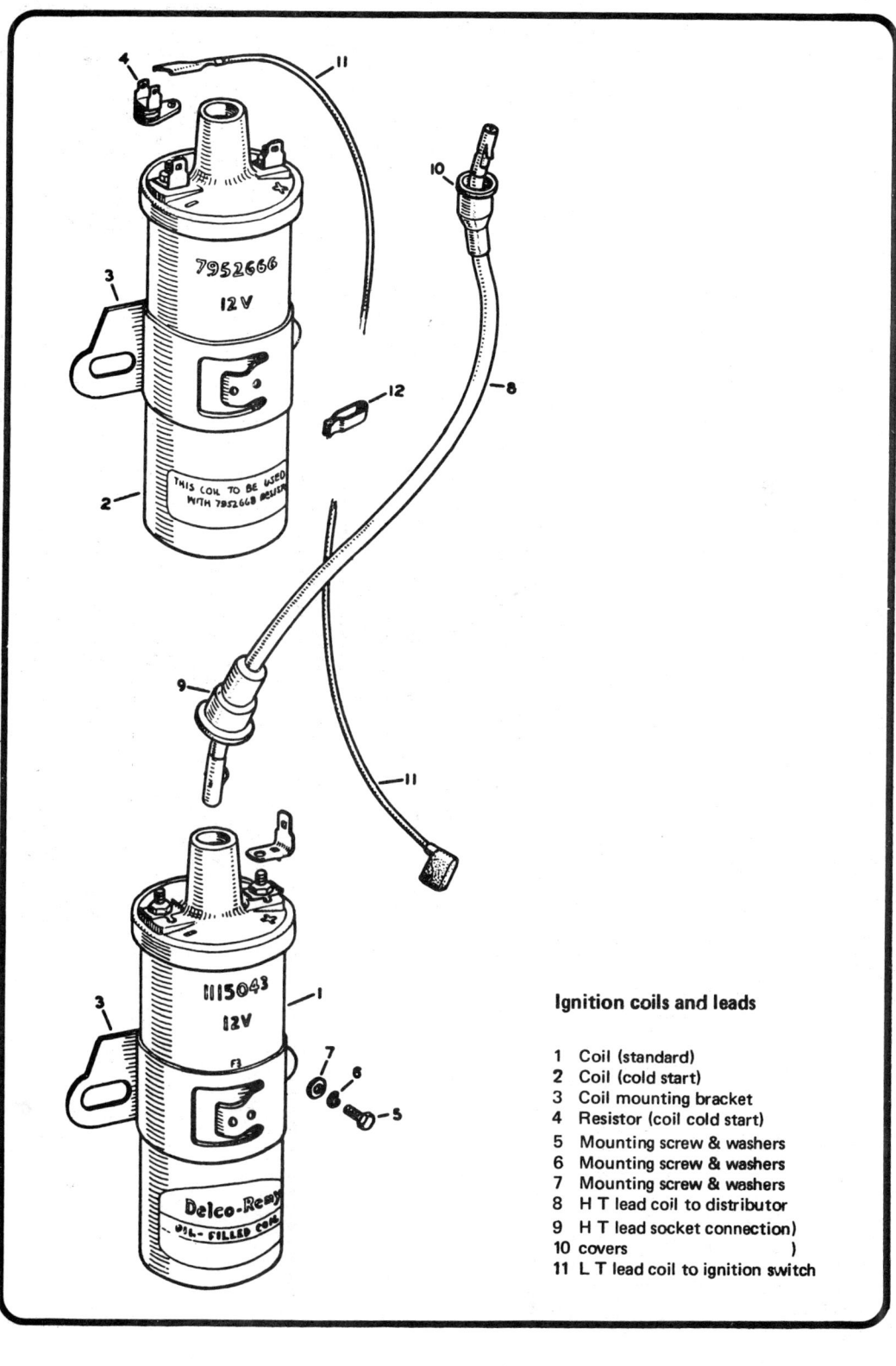

Ignition coils and leads

1 Coil (standard)
2 Coil (cold start)
3 Coil mounting bracket
4 Resistor (coil cold start)
5 Mounting screw & washers
6 Mounting screw & washers
7 Mounting screw & washers
8 H T lead coil to distributor
9 H T lead socket connection)
10 covers   )
11 L T lead coil to ignition switch

The car will not start or stops on the road and will not re-start

Possible Fault	Check and Remedy
Battery engine-to-chassis earth connection	Check condition and tightness of engine-to-chassis earth braided wire lead which goes from the front of the engine to the chassis frame.
Starter motor defective	If all the above fail to produce any improvement the starter motor is at fault and will have to be removed and repaired or replaced. The car can be push or tow started.

Symptom The starter motor turns the engine which will not fire and run

Possible Fault	Check and Remedy
Ignition system failing to supply the necessary spark at the plugs	1 Check that the four plug leads are securely fixed at the distributor and plug ends and that the lead from the centre of the distributor to the coil is also secure. If these are in order, next check that the smaller wires are securely fixed to the coil (2 terminals). If these are in order pull the heavy (HT) lead from the centre of the distributor. Keeping your fingers away from the metal end, hold it about 1/8 - 1/4 inch from the engine block. If the engine is now turned at the starter a spark should jump from the end of the lead. If you have no one to operate the starter key you can switch on the ignition and press the rubber button on the solenoid switch to operate the starter yourself under the bonnet. If a later solenoid switch is fitted there will be no button so you will need help to operate the key switch. 2 If there is no spark from the lead move on to paragraph 3. If there is a spark from the lead replace it in the distributor cap and pull one of the other leads from a plug. If the end is shrouded in an insulated cap, so that it is difficult to get at the metal end of the lead, remove

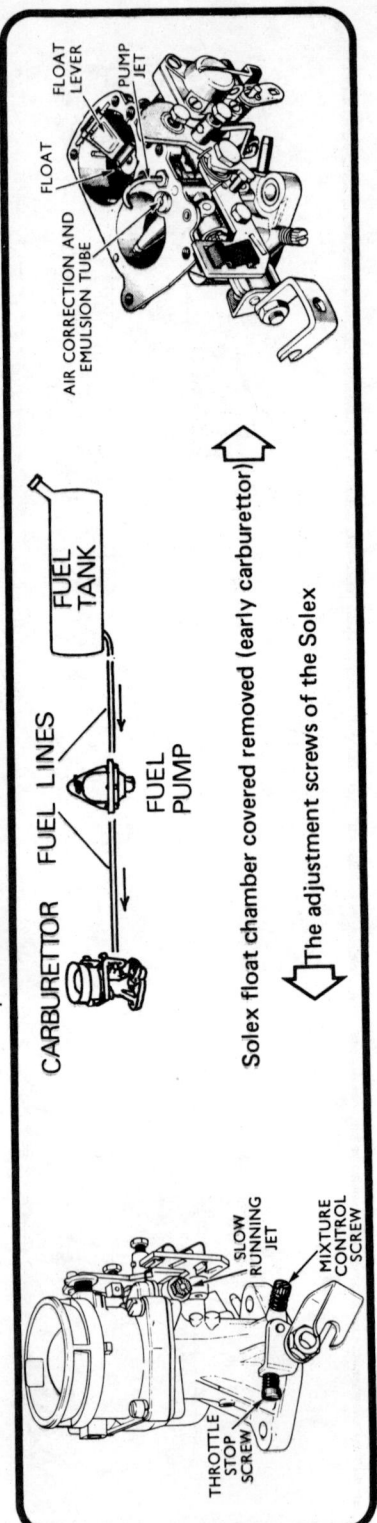

CARBURETTOR   FUEL LINES

FUEL TANK

FUEL PUMP

Solex float chamber covered removed (early carburettor)

The adjustment screws of the Solex

AIR CORRECTION AND EMULSION TUBE

FLOAT

FLOAT LEVER

PUMP JET

THROTTLE STOP SCREW

SLOW RUNNING JET

MIXTURE CONTROL SCREW

The car will not start or stops on the road and will not re-start

the spark plug from the engine and refit to the end of the lead. If you always carry a spare plug you can save yourself the trouble of undoing one from the engine. You want to see if a spark will jump the same as it did for the coil lead, so hold the end of the wire (if bare) near the engine or rest the outside of the spark plug on metal (not near the spark plug hole). Turn the engine again at the starter. If there is a spark, go to the other possible area (fuel system) which affects the starting. If there is no spark at the plug then there must be a fault between the end of the coil lead and the end of the plug lead. Take off the distributor cap by springing back the clip at each side. Look at the rotor arm and check that the spring contact blade on the top is intact and that there is a gap between the end of it and the rotor arm of at least ¼ inch. Carefully bend it upwards if the gap is less. Look inside the cap itself and see that the four contact terminals and the centre terminal are completely clean and free from moisture or corrosion. Scrape them with a knife or nail file if in any doubt, likewise the tip of the rotor arm. Check also that the cap is not broken or cracked. Having checked and remedied any faults in the distributor cap replace it and see if a spark is obtainable at the plug. If there is still no spark at the end of the plug lead go back to make quite sure that there is one at the coil lead into the distributor. If you are checking the spark using the plug attached to the lead, examine the plug carefully and see that the points gap is roughly correct (two thicknesses of the cover of this book) and that it is not broken or clogged with deposits. If in doubt try another plug and plug lead.

3 With no spark at the coil HT lead remove the distributor cap by snapping back the clip at each side. Look at the contact points and see if they are open or closed. If open, you should be able to slide a piece of paper between them. Kick the engine with the starter until they are closed. Leave the ignition switch on and with something non-metallic such as a sliver of wood or a plastic ball pen (with cap on) push the points open, at the same time holding the coil lead about ¼ inch from the engine block. If there is a spark now, then the points need cleaning and regapping. If there is a very noticeable spark at the points but none at the HT lead then the coil or condenser is unserviceable and needs replacement. If not, then pull the small lead off the terminal at the coil marked '+' or 'SW'. With the ignition switched on, lightly brush the metal tag against a bare metal part nearby. It should spark. If it does not, then you have electrical difficulties somewhere between the ignition switch and the coil. In such cases a temporary remedy can be achieved by running a piece of insulated wire from the '+' terminal of the battery to the '+' or SW terminal on the coil. This has the same effect as switching on the ignition and once the engine is started it will have to be disconnected to stop the engine.

* Note: Where '+' terminals are referred to it assumes that the battery earth is negative (—). If otherwise then the references should be reversed.

The car will not start or stops on the road and will not re-start

No fuel reaching the engine

First check that there is petrol in the tank; if the gauge is suspect, dip the tank with a clean piece of stick or wire. Assuming that the tank has fuel in it, remove the air cleaner as described in the appropriate service and look into the carburettor air intake. Get someone to depress the accelerator pedal quickly, once. The fuel pumped into the carburettor choke tube should be seen and smelt. If it is, then the chances are that the engine has probably already been flooded by too much pumping of the accelerator pedal. In such a case, push the accelerator pedal slowly to the floor and keep it there, using no choke and turn the engine on the starter until it fires. On high performance engines fitted with a Stromberg carburettor there is no such pump fitted. In such cases do not attempt to dismantle or touch any part of the carburettor which is easily put out of balance if you are not familiar with them. Check the fuel pump as described later in this section and, if this is satisfactory, call for qualified help to attend to the carburettor. If no fuel can be seen or smelt, disconnect the fuel line from the fuel pump at the carburettor. Place a container under the disconnected pipe and get someone to turn the engine over on the starter. A good spurt of petrol should come from the fuel pump every second revolution of the engine. If no fuel spurts out do not automatically assume that the pump is at fault, but disconnect the fuel tank to fuel pump pipe and blow

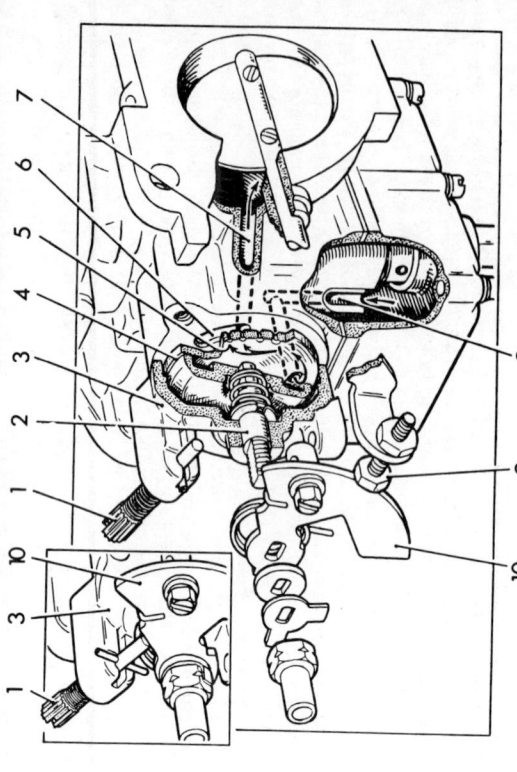

Stromberg 150 CD carburettor - starting operation

1 Starter assembly travel adjuster
2 Starter assembly disc valve spindle
3 Starter assembly outer housing
4 Starter assembly disc valve
5 Metering holes in disc valve
6 Port feed by metering holes in disc valve
7 Fuel feed from port (6) to throttle bore
8 Fuel supply drilling to starter assembly
9 Fast idle speed adjustment
10 Fast idle cam

the inset shows the normal position of the stop (1)

The car will not start or stops on the road and will not re-start

down it to check that it is clear to the tank. If it is clear hold a finger over the pump inlet and get someone to turn the engine on the starter. If the pump is all right a sucking should be felt on the finger as the vacuum operates in the pump. If this is not felt the pump is faulty and must be repaired or replaced. If suction is felt, it is possible that the pump is full of dirt thereby preventing it delivering fuel to the outlet pipe. To clean, service the pump as described in the appropriate section of Routine Maintenance, Page 38. If it has been established that the fuel pump is working and still no fuel appears in the carburettor then it can be assumed that the fault lies in the carburettor itself. If you are not familiar with the internal working of a carburettor you would be advised to call for qualified assistance. For those who are familiar, it is sufficient to say that if the fuel pump is known to be feeding correctly and yet the carburettor accelerator pump is not delivering into the choke tube, then the carburettor float chamber must be empty due to a sticking float or needle valve. To remedy this, the top half of the carburettor will need removal (fixed choke versions on standard models) or the float chamber removed from underneath the Stromberg (variable choke) carburettor.

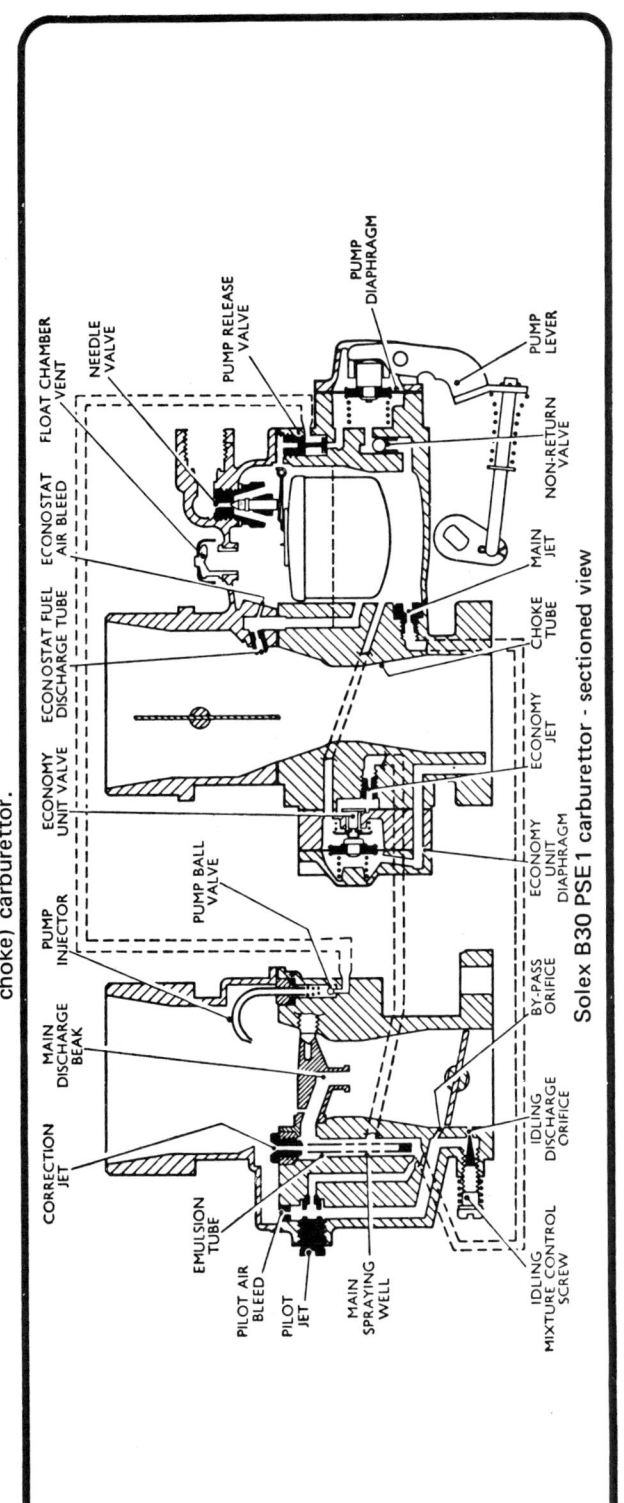

Solex B30 PSE1 carburettor - sectioned view

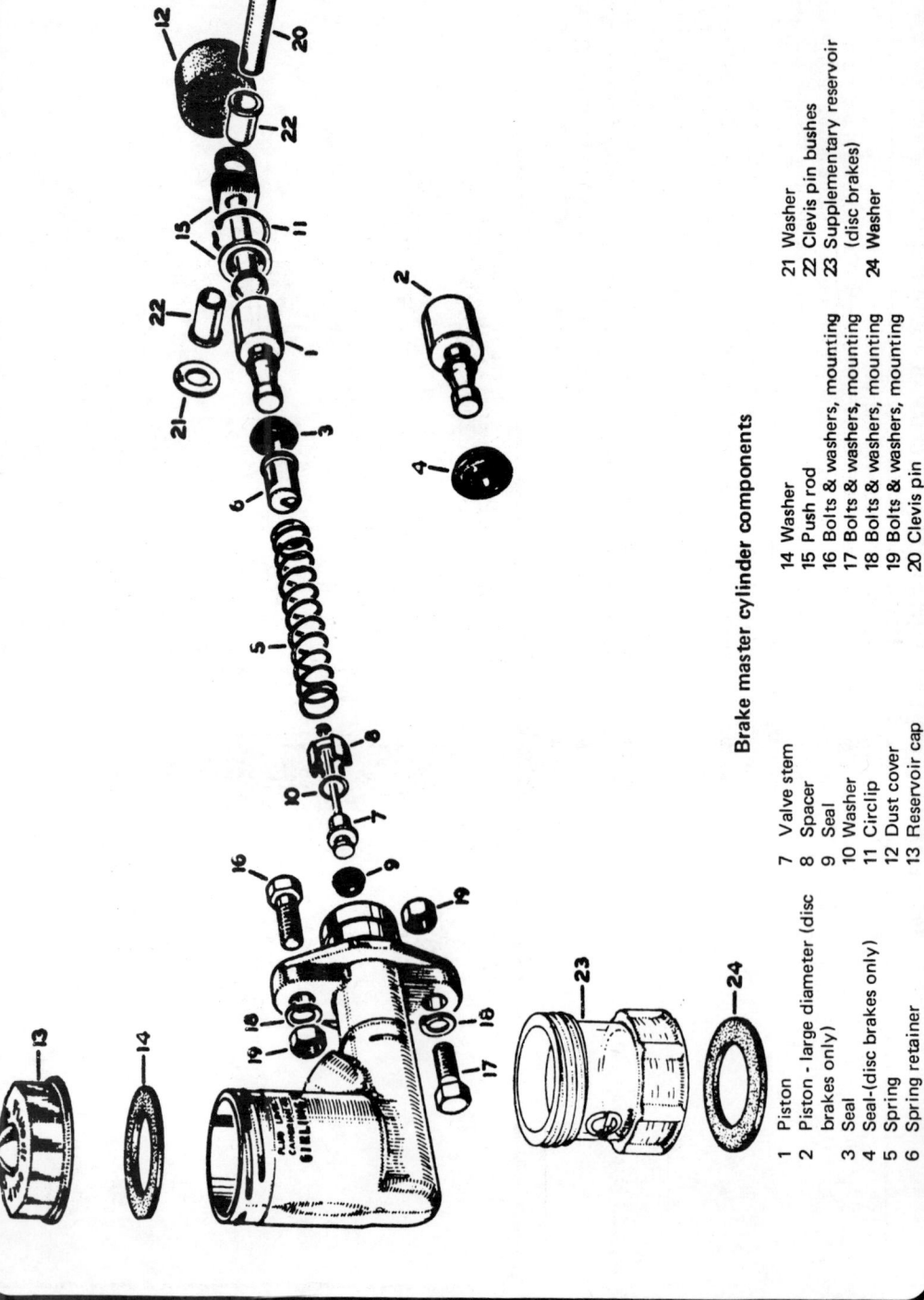

Brake master cylinder components

1 Piston
2 Piston - large diameter (disc brakes only)
3 Seal
4 Seal-(disc brakes only)
5 Spring
6 Spring retainer
7 Valve stem
8 Spacer
9 Seal
10 Washer
11 Circlip
12 Dust cover
13 Reservoir cap
14 Washer
15 Push rod
16 Bolts & washers, mounting
17 Bolts & washers, mounting
18 Bolts & washers, mounting
19 Bolts & washers, mounting
20 Clevis pin
21 Washer
22 Clevis pin bushes
23 Supplementary reservoir (disc brakes)
24 Washer

Emergency - Brakes Inoperative

Symptom Pedal travels right to the floor with little or no resistance and brakes are virtually useless

Possible Fault	Check and Remedy
Bad leak in hydraulic system resulting in considerable loss of fluid and pressure or failure of internal pressure seals	This fault is usually rather sudden and if you are lucky enough not to have hit anything, do not under any circumstances, attempt to drive the car any further. Apart from the danger you will be breaking the law. Call a breakdown vehicle and get the job done professionally, making sure that the braking system is thoroughly tested after repair. Do not drive the car. There is no 'road side' remedy.

Symptom Brakes pull the car to one side when applied

Possible Fault	Check and Remedy
Contamination of the brake shoes due to oil or grease causing brakes on one side to be less efficient	Remove all brake drums to examine shoes. Change shoes if necessary and repair source of contamination.
Partial or complete seizure of one or more hydraulic wheel cylinders resulting in the brakes on one side not doing their share of the work	Jack up both front wheels together and try brakes to see if one wheel is locked sooner than the other. Repeat with back wheels. Have the whole hydraulic system inspected and repaired if suspect.
Brake shoe linings (or disc pads) worn out on one side before the other	Renew linings and have all hydraulics checked for possible seizure of wheel cylinder(s).

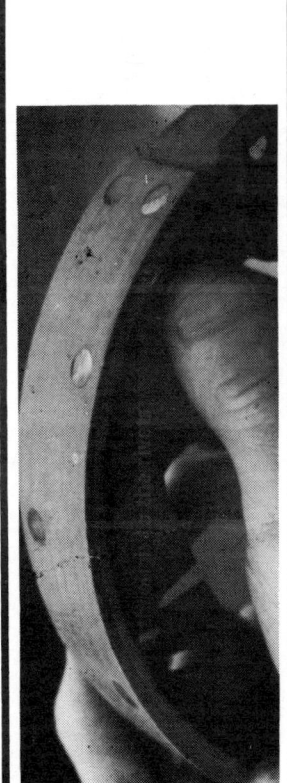

Badly worn brake lining through to the rivets

Emergency - Steering Poor

Symptom Steering is stiff or tends to wander about and the car is difficult to steer properly

Possible Fault	Check and Remedy
Provided the tyre pressures are correct and the steering and suspension units are not damaged as a result of a crash or hitting kerbs and so on, then the fault will be due to wear or impending seizure. If the car is serviced regularly and properly, according to the schedule, the 'sudden' failures which could occur between services are:	If the condition occurs whilst driving on the road, slow down and get to a garage without delay so that a check may be made on the general safety of the steering. Immediate repair may be essential in the interests of safety.
1 Seizure of either of the two track rod ball joints. These are sealed and if not found to be slack on inspection are assumed in order. They can, however, sieze up but this a rarity.	
2 Fracturing of either of the two rubber concertina 'boots' on the steering gear. This would result in all the oil draining out and if this went unnoticed the steering rack and pinion gear would eventually stiffen and possibly seize completely.	
3 Failure of the front wheel bearings.	

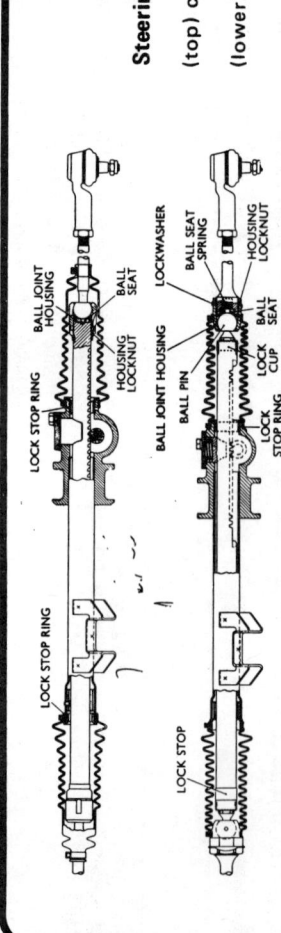

Steering gear assembly cross-section

(top) cam gear,

(lower) Burman

Emergency - Clutch Not Working

Symptom Clutch pedal drops down to the floor

Possible Fault	Check and Remedy
The cable is broken or has become detached at one end or the other	If driving along take your foot off the accelerator pedal immediately, knock the gear lever into neutral and stop. Switch off the engine. We hope you have read this before the situation occurs! By looking underneath the car at the point where the cable joins the clutch operating lever it will be apparent whether the cable is broken or the adjuster nut merely detached - if a broken cable, it is not an easy quick repair so assistance will be needed.

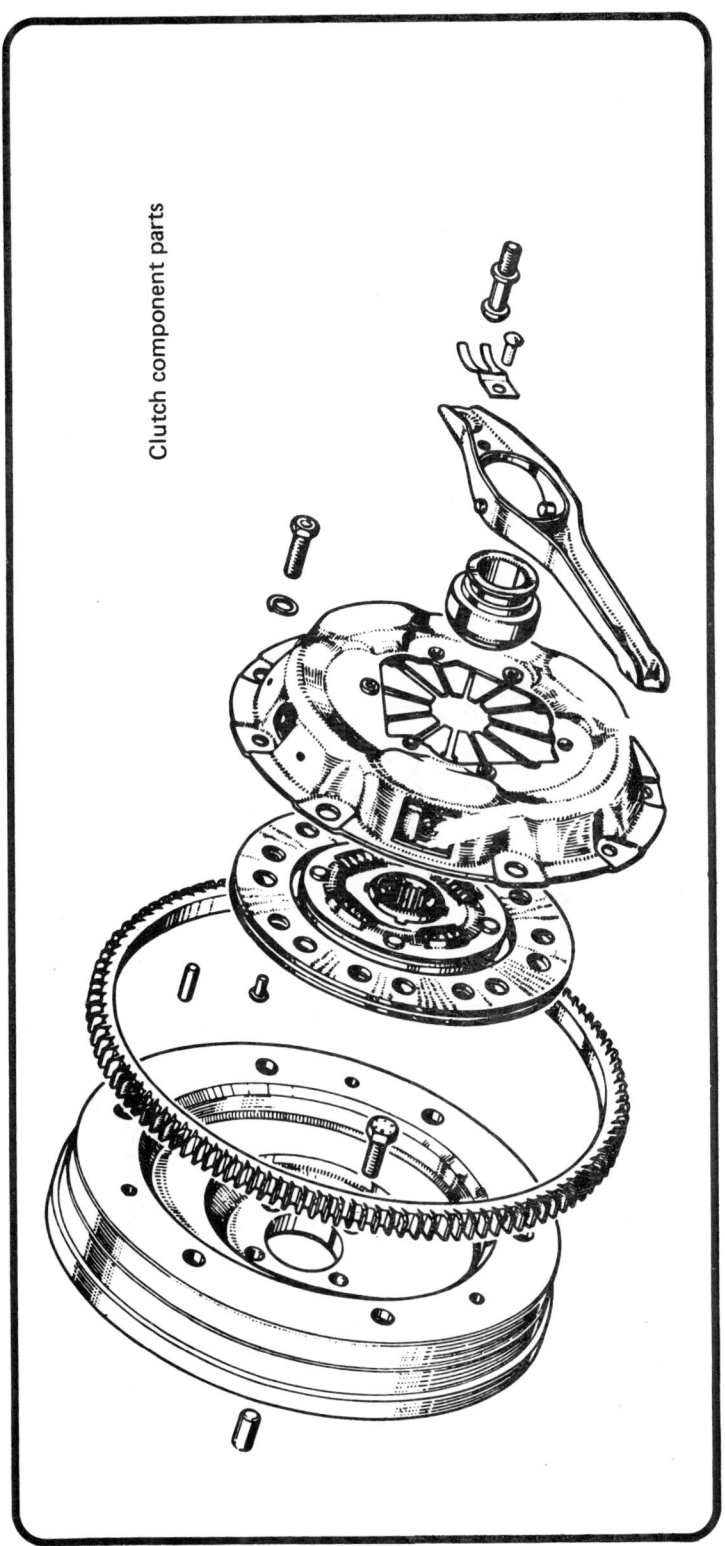

Clutch component parts

Emergency - Lights

Symptom No lights come on at all when switch is operated but other electrical components work

Possible Fault	Check and Remedy
Faulty light switch or broken wire	Electrical faults of this type are very difficult to trace, particularly at night. Check that all visible leads to the headlights, side lights and switches are intact. Be especially careful not to knock connectors off when feeling for loose or hot wiring. Use the wiring diagram to help you identify the relevant wires but if in any doubt do not touch them as you may make final remedy more difficult. Call in a garage who should at least be able to fix a temporary repair. It is dangerous to proceed at night, even very slowly, without lights. You may be able to see - but cannot always be seen.

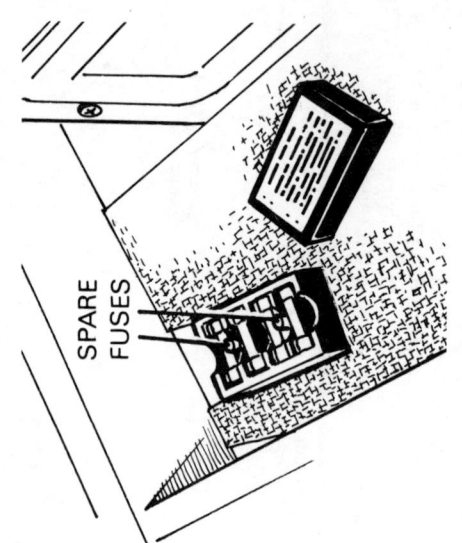

SPARE FUSES

Fuse box located on engine side of shuttle

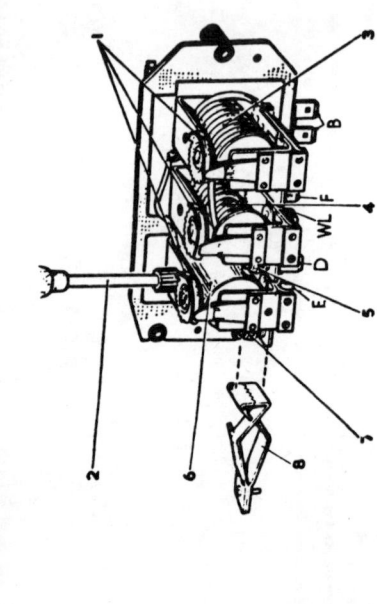

The Lucas RB340 control box with cover removed

1 Adjustment cams
2 Tool for setting adjustment
3 Cut-out relay
4 Current regulator
5 Current regulator contacts
6 Voltage regulator A
7 Voltage regulator contacts
8 Clip to close points manually

Faults and Difficulties - Engine and Associated Features

Symptom Ignition warning light comes on (or does not go out) whilst engine is running above idling speed

Possible Fault	Check and Remedy
Slack or broken fan belt	Adjust or fit new fan belt.
Generator or control box malfunctioning	If the battery is in good condition you can get home provided distance is not great and lights and electrical accessories are not used too much. The engine should not be stopped and started more than absolutely necessary. The generator and control box should be checked before the battery goes flat. If the fault is in the generator it could be quite minor but will get more serious the longer it is left unchecked.

Fan belt tension — Arrows indicate adjustment nuts and bolts, also play on belt at midway point between pulleys.

Faults and Difficulties - Engine and Associated Features

Symptom Green warning light comes on (or fails to go out) when engine is running above idling speed

Possible Fault	Check and Remedy
Lack of oil pressure indicated due to either lack of oil, failure of oil pressurisation internally, or a faulty pressure sender switch	Stop. Check that the oil level in the sump is correct. If it is then either the pressure switch is faulty or the oil pump or some other internal part is not functioning. Do not risk using the engine until the fault is diagnosed. If you do, you run the risk of wrecking it. If the engine needs oil adding, check for signs of serious leaks (with the engine running) before driving further.

Symptom Engine overheats

Possible Fault	Check and Remedy
Slack or broken fan belt	Adjust or fit new fan belt
Loss of coolant due to leaks or under-pressurisation of the system	Examine all hoses and the radiator for signs of deterioration. The radiator pressure cap should be tested at a garage to determine whether it is opening at the correct pressure.
Loss of coolant due to overheating of the engine causing coolant to boil off	Check that the cooling system is clean and not blocked by deposits. Use a chemical cleaner if in doubt. If overheating still occurs engine may need retuning.

Radiator and hose connections

1 Radiator cooling element (matrix)
2 Header tank, inlet pipe & filler neck
3 filler neck
4 Header tank, inlet pipe and filler neck
5 Lower tank, outlet pipe
6 and drain tap boss
7 Lower tank, outlet pipe and drain tap boss
8 Drain tap
9 Overflow pipe
10 Overflow pipe clip
11 Support strap
12 Mounting bolts & washers
13 Mounting bolts & washers
14 Radiator filler cap
15 Top radiator hose
16 Bottom radiator hose
17 Bottom radiator hose (heater fitted)
18 Hose clips
19 Bonnet catch & support
36 stay assembly & landing strip)

Faults and Difficulties - Engine and Associated Features

Symptom Loss of power - fuss and difficulty when starting, poor fuel economy

Possible Fault	Check and Remedy
First it is necessary to classify the car that suffers from the fault. It is either: a) One which is serviced regularly and is kept up to performance standards as a routine b) An unknown quantity as regards past history of mileage, maintenance and treatment in general.	a) The fault has occurred suddenly between services and is not (presumably) as a result of gradual deterioration. In the first instance, therefore, the basic checks and remedies of ignition and fuel given under the failure to start heading should be made. If someone has fiddled with any of the settings of the distributor or carburettor prior to the fall off in performance then it is best to get the engine retuned by a qualified person without delay. b) If the vehicle is an unknown quantity - ie one you may have just acquired - the best thing to do is to have it started on the service 'cycle' as explained in the Routine Maintenance Section and at the same time ask for a specific report on anything which the service shows to be incorrect. You either don't want to know at all (in which case you would hardly buy this book!) or seek reliable information on which to work out what needs to be done to put the vehicle in proper shape. A diagnostic check on special equipment will tell you all. A mass of random checks, adjustments or modifications are quite futile without knowing the state of affairs to begin with.

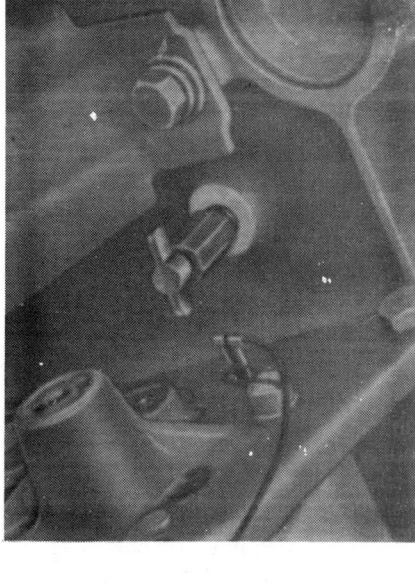

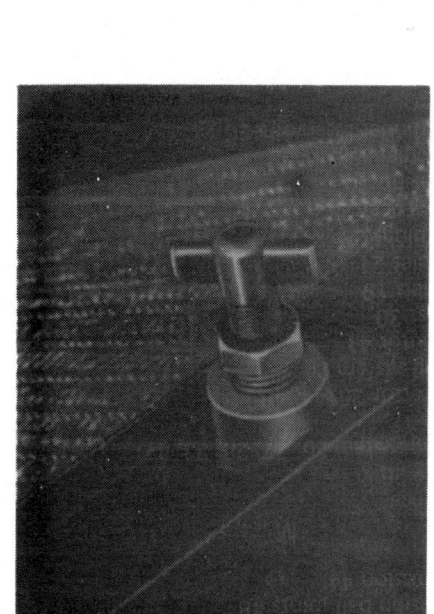

Radiator (left) and cylinder block (right) drain taps

Faults and Difficulties - Other

Symptom When engaging a gear (any gear) when stationary, with the engine running and clutch pedal depressed there is a grinding noise from the gearbox and the car jumps a little

Possible Fault	Check and Remedy
The clutch is not disengaging the drive between engine and gearbox	Check the clutch cable adjustment. The fault indicates that there is excessive movement of the pedal before the clutch starts to disengage. The adjuster screw on the end of the cable under the car should be screwed up so that the operating arm has only ¼ inch of movement before applying pressure to the clutch. If this does not cure the fault then there is something seriously wrong with the clutch itself and it must be removed for repair as soon as possible before further damage is caused. If the car has been standing for a long time unused, the failure of the clutch to disengage may be due to the friction plate sticking or rust on the other surfaces. With luck the tendency to stick will wear off after some running.

Symptom Engine speeds up but the car speed does not increase in proportion

Possible Fault	Check and Remedy
Slipping clutch due to wrong adjustment or excessive wear	Ensure that the clutch cable adjustment is correct as described in the previous paragraph. It will be necessary to unscrew the adjuster nut to correct the play in this condition. If the clutch continues to slip after adjustment then the friction plate is either contaminated or worn out. This is a major repair job involving removal of the gearbox (or engine).

Symptom Excessive noise from engine or gearbox or rear axle or all three

Possible Fault	Check and Remedy
Wear - due to neglected servicing or because the components are nearing the end of their expected life	Replacement or overhaul of the assembly or component. No part lasts for ever. Even with meticulous care and servicing, after 3 service cycles renovations are to be expected. The car is not designed to last longer on the original components unless, of course, the mileage is significantly less than the average.

Index